Courageous

WOMEN OF FAITH

To contact Kathy or for more information visit:
www.kathycrockett.net

Library of Congress Control Number: 2014921075

ISBN 978-0-9862533-0-0

This book is dedicated to my richest blessings on Earth. My husband Steve, who gives me incredible support in all my adventures, and whose deep faith encourages me. His love helps me believe I can do things that I would otherwise not do. Calley and Maddy—my amazing daughters who cheer me on and bless me immeasurably. And my mom, Dr. Lynn Huffman, she has been my mentor, encourager, challenger, wise counsel, and safe place my entire life. Without her this book would not have been complete. She was the final editor for each chapter. I love you all.

Kathy

God can do anything, you know—far more than you could ever imagine or guess or request in your wildest dreams! He does it not by pushing us around but by working within us, his Spirit deeply and gently within us.

Ephesians 3:20 The Message

Contents

Introduction

Kathy Crockett

I've been blessed to meet a lot of people over the years from all walks of life. Whether a CEO of a billion dollar company or an orphan from a third world country, I would find myself riveted by their stories and inspired by their faith through adversity. Often, I would write their experiences, and the lessons I learned from them, in my journals. About a year ago, I sensed that the stories I am blessed to hear and collect show the powerful love of God and are glimpses of His miracles. These accounts need to be shared so others can be encouraged. This realization led to a challenging adventure of reaching out to authors, contacting editors, and learning about book publishing.

It has been such a privilege and honor to be trusted with stories from the women featured in this book. They are very close to my heart. I have shed many tears and said many prayers as I worked with them to formally write about their experiences. In each chapter you will find a compelling story of hope that has arisen out of tragedy, struggle, and pain. It took a great deal for each of them to share in such a public way. These are courageous women of faith. I know their desire is to offer readers hope and encouragement as we all walk together on this journey with our Lord and Savior Jesus Christ.

Will You Believe Me for the Impossible?

Melissa Quayle

My once upon a time began over thirty years ago when I left my home in Arkansas to attend Lee College in Tennessee. It was there that I fell in love with my college sweetheart, Perry. Following college, we worked together in full time ministry for 25 years. After ten years as an associate minister, we were heading to LaGrange, Georgia to start a new full-time pastorate.

I don't know about you, but sometimes I just have to have a whining session with God. He is a big God and He can handle it. Taking this new ministry position meant we had to leave behind our home, our church, and even some of our family. Our daughter, Tiffany, was a sophomore in high school, and our son, Matthew, was a senior. Matthew would be staying behind to complete his senior year. Let me tell you, as a mother, I was not handling that well. So, in my whining session, I was open and frank with God about how I was feeling. "God, I feel like Abraham. I feel like you are asking me to lay everything that I love on an altar and sacrifice it. You are asking me to leave my church, my friends, and my family. Asking me to lay my son on the altar and give him up— asking me to put a knife to everything that I love and leave everything that is familiar." And God answered me so sweetly. *What did I do for Abraham?* "You gave him a ram." *Everything you need will be in that ram.*

So we made the move. Perry had seemed to be a little under the weather for the previous several months;

he had developed a cough, but the doctors accredited that to allergies. We went to see a specialist, and an x-ray revealed something in his lungs. They felt fairly certain it was a chronic disease known as sarcoidosis, but they wanted to do a biopsy to be sure. Because Perry was under the anesthesia, I met with the doctor after the biopsy.

I'll never forget walking into that room by myself and seeing the doctor sitting there, pale, with his head in his hands. "I don't know how to tell you this Mrs. Keyt, but your husband has stage 3 lung cancer."

It was like an out of body experience. Cancer hadn't even been on the radar. All I could think was, "This really can't be us. He's never smoked a day in his life."

The doctor went on, "Does your husband take bad news well?" I could tell that he did not plan to be the one to break the news to Perry. So, the task fell to me.

As we were leaving the parking garage, Perry asked me what the doctor had said. I told him that we would talk about it later, and he stopped me, saying, "No, I want you to tell me right now." So, I had to tell the love of my life that he had stage 3 lung cancer. That was eight days after our first Sunday at our new church.

On our way home we called Perry's mom to tell her. Some dear friends of ours that had become almost surrogate grandparents to our kids were at our house when we told the kids what was happening.

Dan, our adopted grandfather, spoke a profound truth to our family in that moment. "You know what? No matter what name this has, we know that everything has to bow to the name of Jesus."

So we made the decision as a family that we were not going to walk in fear. I remember looking at my kids and saying, "I am so thankful that God trusts us enough to walk this journey." My wonderful mother-in-law told me she understood exactly what I meant, but if I said that in public, people would think I was crazy. But I meant it. I still mean it today; I just say it through a lot more tears now.

One of our first questions was why God would bring us to minister to a new church only to have Perry be diagnosed with cancer. We believed with all of our hearts that this situation was just going to be another way for God to receive glory.

I was adamant about how we were going to approach the situation. I told people, "If you can't stand in faith with us, I do not want you calling and speaking doubt or fear to my husband."

Perry joked with the church at one point, "You'll have to excuse my wife. She is a bulldog/rottweiler dressed as a poodle."

The church, even though we were new, prayed with us, stood with us, and believed with us. So, we held fast, rock-solid in our faith, believing that Perry was going to be miraculously healed.

Perry had never smoked, and there was no history of cancer in his family. It truly made no sense, but God had promised me that He would provide everything I needed in that ram. So, you had better believe that this girl began studying Abraham. I had heard his story preached all of my life. I had studied about him, and even taught about him before. Yet, I needed to know more about him. How in the world could a man take a knife and sacrifice his own promise?

Romans 4:19-21 Without weakening in his faith, [Abraham] faced the fact that his body was as good as dead—since he was about a hundred years old—and that Sarah's womb was also dead. Yet he did not waver through unbelief regarding the promise of God, but was strengthened in his faith and gave glory to God, being fully persuaded that God had power to do what He had promised. Faith is not ignoring the facts. Faith is when you believe God with undaunted perseverance, despite the fact that everything around you is telling you something different. You see, I never denied that my husband had cancer. But I believed the truth much more than I believed the facts. The truth to which I held fast was my faith and my trust in God.

Genesis 22:1-2 Some time later God tested Abraham. He said to him, "Abraham!" "Here I am," he replied. Then God said, "Take your son, your only son Isaac, whom you love, and go to the region of Moriah. Sacrifice him there as a burnt offering on one of the mountains I will tell you about." Abraham was human just like us; he had feelings and emotions. He had this promise that God had given to him, and now God was telling him, *I want this son that I have given to you back.* Imagine. You never even asked for this promise. Remember, God is the one that told Abram, *Go out and look at the stars in the sky. As many stars as you can see, so shall be your descendants.* Abraham never asked to be the father of many nations, but God chose him, and now God is asking for that promise back.

The January before Perry's diagnosis in September, I was sitting in a special time of worship with my head bowed, minding my own business. Then, out of nowhere, I vividly heard God ask me a question: *Will you believe me for the impossible?* It wasn't loud, but it was loud enough that I literally looked up to see if anyone heard it. Nobody was looking up except me. I was so excited; I felt like I had been hand-picked when He asked that question. The next morning, reality hit me. In order to believe in the impossible, I would have to be in an impossible situation. I just had no idea what lay ahead of me.

During Perry's chemo, we were living in LaGrange, and his treatments were in Cobb County, which meant we had to drive quite a ways for every treatment. This was when gas was over $4 a gallon. There was one month during that time that we spent over $1800 for gas for our car. Our old house still had not sold, so we were maintaining two homes. And to top it all off, I was away from my son. So, I was getting a little panicked. I thought maybe God needed reminding of everything we were dealing with. As I started to pour out my problems to him, I said, "God, what are you doing? This makes no sense to me, it makes no sense!" Then He said a phrase to me that still to this day brings tears to my eyes. *Melissa, I thought you said you wanted to look like me.*

Genesis 22: 5 [Abraham] said to his servants, "Stay here with the donkey while I and the boy go over there. We will worship and then we will come back to you." This is my favorite passage in the whole story. Abraham was my example when I was desperate to know how to walk this walk of faith. Even though God was asking for his son, he still responded with *we will worship*. You see, he loved God more than he loved his promise. When Abraham said *we will come back*, he was saying "God you have asked for my promise, yet I am still going to worship you. Somehow, I will still come back with my promise." When Isaac asked Abraham, "Where is the sacrifice?" Abraham told him that God would provide. He was looking eye to eye with his promise, and he said that the Lord would provide.

During Perry's illness, I can tell you that the man walked a life of worship. When the pain was too great, he would have to try and sleep in our recliner, so I would lie on the couch to sleep. If I woke up at any point, I would look over and see him with tears streaming down his face, listening to music on his headphones and worshipping. In the fourteen months following his diagnosis, Perry only missed one Sunday of preaching. As the chemo destroyed his body, we were in and out of the hospital all the time. Many Sundays, I would have to get him dressed in order to get him to church. Some days, he was so weak that he had to sit in a chair to preach. He had a banner made for our church that said "Don't let what's wrong with me stop me from worshipping what is right with Him."

I can't tell you how thoroughly I believed my husband would be healed. I was convinced he was going to live. We were building a house with the contingency of selling our house back in Cobb County. I would take him out there and prophesy what our future was going to look like. I told him that someday we were going to be out there with all of our grandbabies. We had picked out all the cabinets, granite, and carpet. I had scriptures picked out that we were going to write on the floor of each room. I was convinced that he was going to be healed. I remember being on the phone with my brother; he was the only one for whom I did not feel that I had to be strong. I was crying and telling him how tough things were, yet, I can vividly remember telling him, "Barry, the good news is that at least I don't have to worry about being a widow." I was convinced.

On November 26, 2008, I was still so convinced that Perry was going to live. Even when we were in ICU, the kids and I were around praying and singing healing scriptures. At 8:30 that morning, when they said that Perry was going to be moved to hospice, I told him, "You and I both know that you are walking out of hospice." I was thoroughly convinced. I was lying in bed with him when he began to get really bad. I had become very close to the ICU nurse, and she had asked if I wanted her to stay. She was on the right side of me, and I was next to him in the bed when he quit breathing. I asked her, "Is this it?" and she told me yes. But even then, I wasn't asking if he was dead. I believed he was going to come back; that's how convinced I was.

He didn't come back.

I remember sitting in my son Matthew's lap, crying with Tiffany, my daughter, right beside us. I don't know where it came from – I can promise you I am not this big, or this spiritual – but something in my spirit rose up. I got up and got back up on his bed and said, "God, you are the Alpha and the Omega. You are the Jehovah Rapha: the healer of all things. You are Jehovah Jirah: my provider. I will declare this: from this day forward, as for me and my house, we will serve you." I don't know where that came from, but looking back on it now it was as though I had to draw a line in the sand, saying, "Devil, you will not have my children. You will not have my family. You will regret the day you ever touched my family, because we will touch the body of Christ. We will absolutely let people know that you can be crushed, you can be broken, your hopes can be devastated, and you can still come out on the other side." I am so aware that the way I worship is the only way I have remained sane; it is the only way I still have breath in me. In God's presence is the fullness of joy, even in the midst of the greatest of sorrows. I am so convinced of that.

The days after Perry went to be with the Lord consisted of simply putting one foot in front of the other, just getting up every day and doing the tasks before me. We had sold our home in Cobb County the Labor Day before Perry died. So, when he died, we were living in a rental house as the home we were building was being finished. Matthew was off at college. I had to get out of the contract for the house and find a place for my daughter and me to live. So truly, Tiffany and I were homeless when Perry died. The only thing that sustained us was just total belief in God that He would take care of us.

My children will tell you that they both dealt with a lot of shock and disbelief initially. Tiffany especially was really wrestling with fear, a struggle that I had dealt with all of my life. I was talking to her about how God did not give us a spirit of fear and how perfect love casts out fear. Then God began to nudge my heart, and I was thinking, "Yes Lord, I know that perfect love casts out fear, haven't you been hearing me talk about this with Tiffany?" He spoke to me. *No, you have got to know me; I _am_ perfect love. If you know how much I love you, you will walk anywhere I ask you to walk.* If we know his perfect love, we know we can trust him. My love for my kids cannot compare to the love of the Father. He impressed upon my heart that there is no way He will fail to provide us with what we need.

Every event throughout the first year after losing a loved one is difficult to maneuver. Sometimes you put pressure on yourself to do things the way your loved one would have wanted. Or, you make a really big deal about keeping things exactly how they were before in honor or in memory of your loved one. I went through a lot of confusion at first. I knew in scripture it says that Jesus bore our grief, so I didn't know if I was supposed to be grieving or not. Then I would have someone call me and tell me, "Melissa you have got to grieve, or it will show up somewhere else in your body physically." I am a firm believer that the Holy Spirit teaches us things, so I simply began to pray, "I need you to teach me how to grieve."

People with the best intentions would say things that made the ache so much worse. I had so many people say to me, "I know what this feels like." I even had someone send me a sympathy card that said, "I know what this feels like; I lost my dog." All I needed was for people to tell me, "I am sorry. I have no idea what this feels like, but I am so sorry." I needed them to let me have my grief. One of the biggest things that strengthened me and encouraged me was a group of women in my life who had also lost spouses. I was the youngest of the group at age forty-five, but our common experiences bonded us. I would call them and check on them. Pouring my love and encouragement into other people helped me to get my mind off of myself. But I couldn't do that every day. Some days I just didn't have the strength.

When Perry and I got married, we became one. When I lost him, I became a half-person trying to live as a whole person. Every evening when the sun went down, not only did it get dark physically but also there were moments that I just wondered how I was going to keep going. I didn't have a sounding board anymore; I didn't have someone to talk to when I was trying to help my kids. It was the little things I missed. Not just the intimacy, not just not having someone to touch me, but hearing him say, "Do you have your jacket?" I missed the feeling of security when he placed his hand on my back to support me, and having someone to help me put on my coat on as I left a restaurant. People think the first year is hard, the first Thanksgiving, the first Christmas, trying to make new memories on each first holiday without that loved one, and it is. But, I will tell you that the second year was worse. That was when reality hit. Every holiday was no longer a dress rehearsal. This was my life now. I was alone more than I was with someone. There was one holiday season three years after Perry died that I sat on the couch and watched Christmas movies for the whole month of November and half of the month of December. I just didn't have any get up and go. I gave myself permission to do this because I understood that all I was capable of doing on those days was lying on the couch and watching those movies, and that was okay.

I had always heard that a widow would need to allow the Lord to be her husband. I would try to tell myself that and believe it, but I wanted real arms. The enemy would magnify what I didn't have; he would make me feel like a perpetual third wheel or like a round peg trying to fit in a square hole. I had spent the last 25 years of my life being married, and all of my friends were still married. I just didn't fit. People would look at me with concern and pity and say things like "Wow, if that were my husband, I would never marry again," which was easy for them to say as they went home to their husband. Or, I would have someone say, "You know, Jesus will be your husband, and that should be enough" and that same friend would go home to her husband and go away on a special trip with him. I bet I heard hundreds of times from well meaning friends who loved me, "I just hate this - Perry was such an amazing man – and there are not any good guys left out there." I would say, " Well, there is one." I knew my words were powerful. I just had to keep telling myself and reading in scripture that God is the one who said it is not good for man to be alone.

Tiffany was a junior in high school when Perry died, so we had about a year and a half before she went to college. During that time, my kids and I really bonded to each other. Mathew was only a few hours away at college, and he would come to visit often. We were already an incredibly close family, but this experience drew us even closer together. I experienced deep loneliness when the kids moved away. It is a horrible feeling to see the worry in your children's eyes when they are leaving you, to watch them wrestle with the heavy knowledge that no one will be there with you once they back out of the driveway. I struggled with the loneliness, but at the same time I was overwhelmed with concern for my kids. No kids at the ages of eighteen and twenty should have the burden and worry of feeling responsible for something that is not their responsibility.

Genesis 22:9-13 When they reached the place God had told him about, Abraham built an altar there and arranged the wood on it. He bound his son Isaac and laid him on the altar, on top of the wood. Then he reached out his hand and took the knife to slay his son. But the angel of the LORD called out to him from heaven, "Abraham! Abraham!" "Here I am," he replied. "Do not lay a hand on the boy," he said. "Do not do anything to him. Now I know that you fear God, because you have not withheld from me your son, your only son." Abraham looked up and there in a thicket he saw a ram caught by its horns. He went over and took the ram and sacrificed it as a burnt offering instead of his son. So Abraham called that place The LORD Will Provide. And to this day it is said, "On the mountain of the LORD it will be provided." When God fashioned that ram, he fashioned it with horns so that it would be caught in the thicket. It was specifically designed to be a provision for the father of many nations. God's provision for us is powerful.

I can tell story after story of God's provision for us after Perry died. This is one of the sweetest to me. I remember telling a friend that I couldn't keep sleeping under the same bedspread. I didn't want to spend a lot of money, so we went to Sam's Club. I saw one for $185, and even though I didn't need to spend that much, I decided it would do. I went to the check out, and the lady at the cash register asked how I was doing. I told her I was thankful and blessed, and she said the same. She scanned the bedding and it came up $36.01.

She said, "Girl, that is the favor of God."

I touched her on the hand and said, "You have no idea, you have just seen a ram in the thicket." I carried that receipt in my billfold for a while, because it served to remind me of God's provision. The receipt read:

"COMFORTER $36.01"

It was like a love note straight from the Father to me.

I was making my bed one day, when God asked me a question. *Do you know why I picked out your bedding?* I said "No sir." *So you would know you are resting beneath my provision.* I am not making this up; I am not smart enough to make this all up. God wants us all to know that we are resting under his provision. Abraham and Isaac were walking that road of obedience up one side of mountain, while their provision was walking up the other side. God wants us to know that He provides; Psalm 34 talks about him being our deliverer, close to the brokenhearted. How many of us are guilty of trying to deliver ourselves? We try to get ourselves out of our situations, out of our circumstances, and all the while God is asking us like He asked me that morning during worship: *Will you believe ME for the impossible?*

About a year after losing Perry, the Lord spoke to my heart. *You need to embrace your singleness.* It made my stomach drop. I knew marriage was in my future, and so his words confused me. He went on to say, *Be the best you you can be.* I began to start trying to make myself a better me. When I would pray over my future spouse, one of the scriptures I would pray was to make me a suitable helpmate. I knew I had prayerfully been a helpmate suitable for Perry for 25 years, yet, I knew my future husband would have different needs with different things in his life.

I was single for a total of five years after Perry passed away. I knew in my heart that I would eventually get married again, and I had talked with my kids at length about it. Tiffany embraced the idea more than Matthew at first, but after Matthew fell in love and got married, he had a better understanding of what I had lost. I was probably ready to start dating about two or three years in, but I didn't want to go out on a date just for the sake of dating. I wanted to be sure it would be with someone who was compatible with me. I went out on a few dates, but it was just not a fit. It was very discouraging, and I often felt that I would just rather be at home. The enemy tried to convince me that finding someone at my age that had the same beliefs that I did and who would love my kids the way I needed him to was impossible. But then my daughter-in-law told me about someone that her aunt Jeanette knew, and told me that they wanted to introduce us.

Jeanette's father was a pilot, and had been hired by a man named Mike to give him some flying lessons for a specific kind of plane. Both being strong believers, the men connected during their time together. As soon as Jeanette heard about Mike, she instantly thought of me. So, of course I trusted my daughter-in-law and Jeanette, and I let them contact Mike for me. He was a little apprehensive at first, because he had had some bad experiences with set-ups, but he went ahead and emailed me. That very same morning as I was working out, I just really had an amazing time with the Lord. Through serious tears and sobbing, I felt like it was the first time I was able to celebrate the Lord as my true husband. I just worshipped him. I said through tears, "Lord, you are the greatest husband I could have dreamed of, the greatest husband I could have asked for." The timing of it all was incredible, and I know without a doubt that it was all God's doing.

Mike poured his heart out to me in his email. He was a retired newspaper publisher. His wife had died of cancer several years before, and that had caused him to lose his faith and become an alcoholic. During that broken time of his life, he had remarried, but that marriage had ended because of his alcoholism. He told me that he was nine years sober, that he had a great love for God, and that he may even sound like a zealot at times.

I laughed and thought, "Wow, you don't know me yet. You just wait." We emailed back and forth for a while and then had a live phone call. After that, we talked pretty often on the phone and skyped. I felt like I was falling in love with him even before I ever met him in person.

Mike flew to Tennessee to see me and meet my kids. I had been very open with my children about Mike, and in our early dating stages I had forwarded all of Mike's emails on to my kids to read. Tiffany and Matthew joined us for the first dinner of his visit. My children are so much a part of me that it is like they are an extension of my own heartbeat, so it was very important that they be included in the process. We had plans to all fly up to Ohio to spend a weekend together. Mike was showing me his plane, an old style, open cockpit Waco biplane. He and I were in the front cockpit, and I saw a plaque on the plane with letters and numbers. I asked him what it was and he told me it was the call letters of the plane. I said, "You are kidding. That is my birthdate and my initials." It was like another one of those precious love notes from God. It was like He was saying, *I've got you. I've had you this entire time.*

Mike asked Matthew and Tiffany for their permission to marry me before he asked me. He told them that he didn't want to ever replace their dad, but that he would like to be whatever they wanted or needed him to be in their lives. Mike and I had flown to Arizona so that I could meet his mom and get her approval. While we were there, we would go out on morning flights. One morning, we were flying over the Sedona mountains and talking about what heaven was going to be like. He asked me, "Would you live with me in heaven as my wife?" and took a ring out of the back seat of the plane. So, we got engaged flying over the Sedona mountains.

We got married on August 31, 2013. It was an amazing outdoor wedding; my son walked me down the aisle, and our kids were the ones who stood with us as our attendants. It was a beautiful day, and we spent it surrounded by some of the most important people in our lives as we began this amazing endeavor.

I like to call Mike my Boaz. I had a list of things I wanted to find in a man before I would remarry. I wanted someone who would be able to travel with me and work with me. At my age, I knew that would be difficult to find, but Mike was retired at an early age. He travels with me, and we minister to people together. We talk to people about preventing disease, staying healthy, and keeping their bodies strong. Another important reason why Mike and I work so well is because we both know how it feels to have lost someone. All of our children have lost a parent. When I made my list of what to look for in my Boaz, I figured there were some items on there that were wishful thinking. Kind of like as a kid when you circle all the things you wish you could have out of the Sears and Roebuck Christmas catalog, even though you know there are some things that you will never get. But once again, I underestimated God's incredible provision. Not only did I get everything on my list, it's like I got the whole catalog.

I never dreamed that my once upon a time would take the twists and turns that it did. I'm not the same woman that I was seven or eight years ago, but I praise God for that. I am not going to tell you that it did not rock my world when Perry died. He was not at my son's wedding. He was not at my daughter's. He will not be there for our grandchildren. But, every trial that I have been through, that my family has been through, God has used to his glory. He has strengthened me to be a voice in the wilderness for others who are struggling. God has faithfully sustained me and provided for me every step of my journey, and he continues to fulfil his promises to me daily. I don't know what kind of trial you are going through. It may be way tougher than mine. But I can promise you, I am a testimony that God will love you and will never leave you. He will heal those broken places. When you are facing an impossible situation you are either going to stand in faith, or you are going to stand in fear. In fear, you are convinced you cannot pull through. In faith, you are confident in God to control the situation, because He is I AM, our perfect love who casts out fear. *Everything you need will be in that ram.*

About the Author

"Be joyful in hope, patient in affliction, faithful in prayer," from Romans 12:12, has been the life-long foundational principle for Melissa Keyt Quayle. Born and raised in Blytheville, Arkansas, Melissa left home after graduating from high school to attend college at Lee University in Cleveland, Tennessee. While at Lee, she met her husband Perry. After graduating she and Perry spent 25 years in full time ministry in Michigan, Texas and Georgia until Perry's death in November of 2008.

After her husband's death, she returned to Atlanta to raise her two children and then moved three years later to Cleveland to care for her aging father. In 2009, she started her own business with the Juice Plus+ Company and has risen quickly in the ranks to the position of Qualifying National Marketing Director.

In early 2013, Melissa met her present husband Mike, a retired newspaper publisher. They married later that year and together they operate their Juice Plus+ business and travel extensively for business and pleasure.

Melissa is a frequent guest speaker at church and women's events to inspire audiences wherever she travels with her Christian messages of faith and hope.

The Quayle's continue to reside in Cleveland and are faithful members of The Westmore Church of God.

Where, O death, is your victory?
Where, O death, is your sting?
1 Corinthians 15: 55

Joyce Carrell

~

A woman sits alone in the doctor's office. The hum of the air vent is the only sound that can be heard, and it is not enough to drown out the confusion. The woman's name is Joyce Carrell, and her doctor has just told her that she has ovarian cancer. Her thoughts instantly race with questions: *How could I have this diagnosis when I have been living such a healthy lifestyle? Am I contagious? Will I die fighting the same disease my sister-in-law did?*

~

If you haven't met me personally, you most likely know someone who has. I'm quite popular, notorious for bringing a whole new meaning to "divide and conquer." First, I attack your body. I'll make your cells keep dividing and multiplying until they virtually turn your body against you. I can make even the strongest person fall to his knees in weakness. Then, I attack your loved ones. I'll make them feel a plethora of emotions ranging from anguish to fear as they watch your suffering and realize their helplessness in the matter. Lastly, I attack your perspective. The invincibility you used to feel when you thought your life would go on forever will instantly be replaced with fear that your life could end at any fleeting moment. Yes, you can fight me, and you might even win. But the truth is, whether you get rid of me or not, I will change your life forever.

However, I must say that I have seen many faces and fought many battles in my time, but in all my years, there have been none quite as enigmatic to me as Joyce Carrell.

~

Joyce examines herself in the mirror. She tries to smile, but the sores in her mouth cause her too much pain to do so. She wants to put on her favorite dress, but the abrasions on her body say otherwise. Instead, she puts on loose clothing, which has become her regular attire since she started chemotherapy. She thinks back to the first weeks of her early treatment; things seemed so easy then. For the most part, she was able to continue her regular life activities and she had very few side effects. The results were looking hopeful and the cancer appeared to be gone for a short time. Then the cancer returned; the treatments got more intense. Now, Joyce has come to terms will her illness. The foot sores and burning after even the shortest of walks are a constant reminder that she can no longer do the things she used to.

~

I have come to the conclusion that the best way to discourage a person is to give them a seemingly sure sign of hope before taking it away. This is exactly what I did with Joyce. I gave her a false sense of ease by letting her carry out her regular tasks without my interference. I even left for a short while. When I returned, however, I came back stronger than before. I made it hard to ignore my presence. I knew Joyce had a lot of confidence in her physical abilities, and when I made those difficult, she showed brief signs of discouragement. Despite the sores, pain, abrasions, and ulcers, there was a part of Joyce I could not touch: her soul. I thought I broke her spirit, but it turns out I only made it

stronger. There is no doubt she possessed a power bigger than herself, a power that could only come from the spirit of Christ.

~

The resonant chime of the clock penetrates the silence and startles Joyce awake. Surrounding her in the dim-lit office is a pile of books and articles. She checks the time; it's 2 a.m. This is not the first time Joyce has fallen asleep in the middle of studying. In fact, it has almost become part of her daily routine. Joyce treats cancer like she treats every challenge in her life; she studies the issue, formulates a plan, and finds the resources to execute the plan. Her intellect, organization, and leadership help her to take on the task at hand. She spends most of her time researching the best ways to stay healthy. Joyce's research starts to consume her to a point where she feels as if she must always have control. She spends everyday trying to do everything exactly perfectly in hopes that it will make the cancer go away; this only adds pressure and anxiety. One week, Joyce grows so weary of her efforts that she finds herself in a valley of despair. Concerned, Joyce's daughter asks Joyce to stay with her for a few days, and she willingly agrees. The few days Joyce spends with her daughter help her regain her perspective. Joyce's daughter, along with other close friends and family, serve and minister to her. They offer words of encouragement and prayer. Through their servitude, Joyce is reminded of God's truth: He is the one in control. When Joyce goes back to her home, she develops a new life motto, "more of Christ, less of self." Joyce realizes she is not alone in her battle and that she needs to accept God's control and allow other people to help her. She no longer holds herself to unrealistic standards, and she learns to enjoy life without lists, demands, and pressure. Regardless of her latest CT scans, her pain, or the progression of her disease, Joyce rests in God's unshakeable peace.

~

As I got to know Joyce more, I became aware of her strengths and weaknesses. I could see that she was extremely intelligent and analytical. With that, I gave her a false sense of control. I got inside of her mind and made her believe that it was up to her to get rid of me. I hoped that by giving in to her desire for control, I would distract her from God's control. For a while, this technique worked. Joyce succumbed to the pressure of battling me on her own; I had her trapped in a corner feeling overwhelmed and helpless. But then, something odd happened. Joyce spent a few days at her daughter's house, and something in her changed. Instead of trying to have control of the situation, she allowed her daughter, other family members, and friends to help and serve her. They say, "there's strength in numbers," and that was definitely true in this case. I saw Joyce's security in God restored through the prayers and encouragement of others. When she returned from her daughter's house, there was a peace about her that was untouchable. No matter how much I persisted, her faith only seemed to grow stronger.

~

Joyce and her friend Norma sit in silence as they watch the sunrise. They have made a pact to wake up every morning together and ask God what He wants them to do with each day they are given. Norma, like Joyce, is battling cancer.

A while back, Norma was on a long-term work assignment in a Los Angeles California Hospital. She was commuting from East Texas and she was away from her family when her physician, and working colleague, diagnosed her with metastatic head and neck cancer. Norma was rushed to MD Anderson to be treated immediately. From there, the doctors seemed to deliver nothing but bad news. First, Norma's primary tumor could not be identified, so her treatment plan included large doses of radiation. Then, the tumor started growing too fast, so Norma was rushed into surgery. The surgery revealed that the metastasis was no longer contained in Norma's lymph nodes, but that it had spread to the muscles and nerves in her neck and lip. This gave her a stage four diagnosis and a need for chemotherapy. The biopsies of Norma's tongue and removal of her tonsils still failed to reveal the primary tumor, meaning that the doctors had one shot to destroy the cancer before it spread any further.

While she was still in the process of recovering from surgery, Norma had to undergo the most aggressive treatment: daily radiation and weekly chemotherapy. The radiation was so close to her brain that it required her head to be immobilized with a custom fitted mask that screwed to the table so tightly that she could not move her eyelids. The surgical site would bleed each time and her neck became so burned that it was a mass of blisters with peeling and bleeding skin. She had mouth sores so severe that she could not swallow her own saliva. Norma was not able to finish chemotherapy before being admitted to the hospital for blood transfusions. She had to be placed in isolation because her immune system was destroyed. Two years after her diagnosis, Norma was still in recovery when she received bad news about her disabled son. Norma's son, already dealing with severe Cerebral Palsy, was diagnosed with leukemia.

Now, three years later, Norma is here with Joyce. She has overcome much in her life. Her bone marrow is beginning to recover and she is just now getting close to an acceptable white blood cell count and healthy immune system. Her time with Joyce has been a true blessing from God. Joyce and Norma do not go to a normal cancer support group; they do not believe in complaining. Instead, they let the colors of the sunrise pour through the window and remind them of the little things God does each day. They chase God's peace and vow to not go to their graves quietly, but to "run full speed and skid sideways into the grave."

~

I have always been baffled by the idea of friendship. My sole purpose in life is to destroy people and their relationships, and yet, Joyce and Norma only seem to get closer the more I interfere in their lives. I remember the first day I met Norma. She was on a business trip, and I decided to take advantage of her time away from her family and home to create complete chaos. In the midst of the disorder, however, Norma somehow managed to stay composed. Even when the doctors informed her that I was spreading by the moment and that the only way they could get rid of me was through a series of painful treatments and surgeries, Norma remained calm. I was disturbed by the fact that she didn't fear me, and so I tried to enforce my power even more. I decided to introduce myself to her son, thinking that I could discourage Norma if her son had to deal with me on top of the Cerebral Palsy he already deals with on a daily basis. This, however, was not the case. I saw an even stronger friendship form between Norma and her son in spite of me.

Now, as I watch Norma and Joyce wake up every morning together and look at the sunrise, asking God for guidance and direction, I sense a friendship that is based on more than just a common struggle. Norma and Joyce, just like Norma and her son, have a bond that is held together by faith. This faith is so strong that it has created a barrier around their spirits; a barrier that I cannot seem to penetrate for the life of me.

~

Joyce hangs up the phone after what seems like the hundredth phone call she has made today. She looks around the room; her friends and family are surrounding her, all of them wet-faced from tears of joy. *I can't believe it's actually gone*, Joyce thinks to herself, *I can't believe the cancer is actually gone.* The number of people who have prayed and hoped for this moment of victory for her is overwhelming to Joyce. She is in awe of the army of prayer warriors God has blessed her with, and getting to tell them all that she is now cancer free has brought her the ultimate joy. For the first time in what seems like forever, Joyce feels like she will actually get a full and good night's sleep.

~

The thing I like most about celebrations is how short-lived they are. Every celebration of a win must be greeted by a loss at some point. The only way I was able to bear watching Joyce celebrate my departure was the fact that I knew what was coming after. Joyce thought I was gone for good, but I wasn't. I was simply waiting for the right timing to remind her of my presence.

~

Joyce's concentration on her planner is broken by the beeping from the kitchen. Joyce quickly scribbles down one more thing before she puts on her oven mitts and

29

pulls the bread out of the oven. Ever since she found out that her cancer was back, Joyce has spent a lot of her time thinking about service. Even though she is limited, Joyce wants to serve as much as she can. Joyce can no longer pass out the visitor bread at church because she has trouble standing, but she sees that as an opportunity to bake the bread instead. She also keeps track of community events in her planner, and makes an effort to get everyone involved that she possibly can. Joyce replaces her pain and disappointment with appreciation for God's love, and she uses that to motivate herself to reach out and help others.

~

Joyce's acts of servitude in her last few months of living will forever fascinate me. I constrained her physically, and yet, she still found a way to give her church and community everything she could emotionally and spiritually. Her capabilities to do this were like none I have ever seen before. Seeing God's power in action through Joyce almost made me feel remorse for what I was about to do next. *Almost.* But, I had a job to do, and I had every intent of carrying it out. It was time to win the battle against Joyce once and for all.

~

A woman takes a deep breath as she looks out at the crowd in front of her, and then looks down at the paper in her hand. She clears her throat and then opens her mouth to speak:

My name is Carol Bodwell, and I'm from Princeton, Texas, and I'm here to share with you about my special friend, Joyce. I believe one of the things that made Joyce so special is that she made each of us feel so special, and I bet she was your special friend also.

Joyce always called me to do things that I didn't think I was capable of doing. She really gave me a challenge when she told me that she wanted me to do her eulogy (surely this is no surprise that she would have this funeral all planned).

I must have had that look I would get all the times she had me step outside of my comfort zone, because she didn't miss a beat. 'You can do it Carol!'

So here I am. It is all in my heart and soul, but I believe I am going to have to read this to do it out loud. Please be patient if I have to pause.

Joyce had a green thumb not only for plants, but also for people. Joyce was the water and the sunshine for many lives. She had a gift for seeing that seed inside of each one of us that held our gifts and talents, and she picked that seed up and watered and gave it sunlight. She knew just how much water because each plant has different needs, and just how much sun because, once again, each plant is unique; and she would nurture. But, Joyce also expected your best, and she would prune! Once she chose that seed, she tended that new plant as needed. I was one of her many on-going projects. For me, that has been over 30 years. I can only give you my journey with Joyce, but I know as you hear our story you will hear your story with Joyce too.

Our story actually began with Joyce looking for some food to help a family in Princeton, and she contacted me because of the food pantry. Needless to say, because she was always helping people, we were in contact frequently.

The first personal challenge came when she called me one day and said, "I want to offer an exercise class for the community and I want you to teach it."

I said, "But I have never done that."

Joyce was not deterred. "Oh I hear you have good rhythm and a voice that carries (how tactful was that), and I have already found a place to send you to get certified!" This was at a time when very few instructors were even certified and I'm not aware of any town as small as Princeton that even had a community education program, much less, an exercise class. But, Joyce was into wellness way ahead of her time.

Joyce used the community education program to start offering other opportunities to grab those seeds and help people grow. There were Spanish, computer classes, ESL, cooking, gun safety, and all types of art and craft classes from making a rug to painting, parenting, CPR and first aid. But, very biggest was her adult literacy program. I thought *here we go again* as she said, "Carol I want you to teach a GED class."

"What's that?" I asked.

"Oh don't worry, I already have a place for you to go to get certified!" Now, I have to say the most exciting part of that request was we were going out of town and share a room. I couldn't wait to see what Joyce looked like first thing in the morning. She always looked perfect, as if she had just prepared for a photo shoot.

I did scare her though, because the first morning, after four hours of class, we were going to lunch she asked, "Are you okay?"

"What do you mean?"

She replied, "You haven't said a word for four hours, are you okay? You always ask questions!"

"But this time, I don't even know enough to know what question to ask!"

"Oh don't worry, it will all come together," she said, "you can do it!"

Well, she was right. I did great on the teaching part, but that first year I was a mess on the paperwork. However, I'm so thankful for that because instead of Joyce just correcting my paperwork each week, (which would have been much quicker), we started having a working lunch meeting for me to learn how to get it right. You see, funding was affected by the accuracy of these reports, and out of that came our ongoing tradition of our weekly lunches (we were known around town as Lady Di with the half dressed exercise lady). Those lunches continued until she retired and moved to Emory in 2003.

Not only did I eventually learn how to do the paperwork, but also our adult literacy program in Princeton eventually became the largest in the Cooke County co-op in terms of graduates, even larger than Plano, Allen, or McKinney. That was clearly another one of Joyce's visions and successes.

Well, our next adventure is the food pantry lost its housing. "No problem," Joyce says, "you are going to have to write some grants!"

"But Joyce, I've never written a grant, I don't how to do that!"

"Oh, I can teach you. I know you can do it!" she encouraged.

So, she spent an entire weekend with me on a crash course on grant writing and then insisted on proofing each one (tactful again). She could have done it in half the time, but she was a teacher and her role was to empower. You've heard the proverb, "Give a man a fish, feed him for a day. Teach a man to fish, and feed him for a lifetime." Of course, it took time, but the beautiful new building became a reality and is now expanded even more.

But oh, it keeps getting better. I started complaining about the high school drop outs I was seeing at the food pantry and how I thought we should expand the curriculum in Princeton with more career and technology courses to fill in gaps. Now, Joyce didn't like complaining. She was a big believer in if you have a problem, then do something about it.

So she says, "Well, why don't you run for school board?"

"But I've never run for political office before, I'm pretty new in town and I don't know what to do."

"Oh, I will help you find out information and how you would go about doing it, I know you can do it!"

So, here we are 24 years later. I'm still on school board and we have a career and technology center! But it just keeps getting better.

"Joyce, you know, there's a lot of things wrong with the whole school system. We can't do anything about it because it's all coming out of Austin, and we don't have local control." As you can see I had not learned my lesson about complaining and making excuses.

"Oh," Joyce says, "then you just need to go lobby in Austin. I can teach you. You can do it."

And of course, she knew first hand how to lobby. You see, our school had four students killed on a local highway, and she lobbied for years to get that highway widened. Now, instead of two lanes there are five.

At the time that Joyce came to our school district, it was a very, very poor one. There were teachers, principals, and a superintendent; pretty much whatever jobs were left, Joyce did. Her grant writing created many programs that we would not otherwise have had. In addition to the classes in community education and adult literacy, she was a strong advocate with the drug prevention and education programs with D Fy It, red ribbon week, hooked on fishing, as well as after prom parties. There was also the famous baby buggy grant; it bought a van that was used to take pregnant girls to the doctor (and when not in use there, offered needed transportation to other programs).

Joyce did the entire PR for the sesquicentennial as well as take on responsibility for a massive project that resulted in the creation of the Princeton book that is still available today. However, she was disappointed with that project as we only placed second in the state! She also published a newsletter for Princeton that went out during the year, and in those days, it had to be hand done and sent by snail mail.

Joyce wanted to completely utilize the community education building and open it up to the seniors where they could play games and eat together. With Meals on Wheels going out into the community, here comes another grant for the greenhouse and eventually a library was started there.

Joyce was the force behind our Princeton library; she wrote grants and got money for the green thumb program and used seniors to run a part-time library in the community education building. And now, we see a beautiful new facility with a full-time librarian.

Within in her own church home, Princeton Church of Christ, she had numerous ministries that once again touched many lives. From the cradle roll Bible class for little ones up to two years, to teen Bible classes, to mother-daughter retreats, to ladies' Bible class, to pie ministry, to nursing homes, she covered all ages! And not to forget the wonderful parent classes that she facilitated not only at her church, but also in the community for all parents.

I just know that somewhere in my journey and sharing, and through what you have seen yourself, how Joyce was also the wind beneath your wings (and Charlie, you were the wind beneath her wings, thank you for sharing her with us, and Wyatt and Holly, you are the legacy she was proudest of).

That first morning in the hotel room, when she got up with no make up, she was still one classy lady. She had a style that was all her own, extremely trustworthy, intelligent, discreet, and she treated all people with dignity and respect. One person said, "She was my conscience," and I am pretty sure that is true for most of us. She brought out the best in us, for she only permitted the best of what she and others could do to be associated the name of Princeton ISD and its community.

Our community has missed Joyce so much since she left us in 2003. But, she has left her mark in tangible ways that we see everyday, from five lanes on Highway 380, to the new food pantry, to our Princeton library, to the Senior Center and Meals on Wheels, to Community Education programs, to drug programs, to the Career and

Technology center, yes, you can see all these physical marks of her visions and tenacity. But, there is no way to measure the gift of her spirit. At some time and place, there were many of us who were broken mentally, physically, emotionally or spiritually, and she healed us.

Since 2003, Joyce and I have met up on a regular basis and had the gift of more time together. Last month was our last visit and guess what, it was the same as our very first visit over 30 years ago."

~

As much as I would love to tell you that I won, and that this whole ordeal is a victory story for me, it isn't. When Joyce lost her life fighting me, I thought that I had triumphed over her for sure. But, the fact that she's gone and yet, the fact that I can still feel her, tells me otherwise. Joyce Carrell bewilders me, she has from the moment that she gave God control over her life. Descartes once said, "I think, therefore, I am," and if that's true, then Joyce was truly the form of God. What I mean by this is that it was so apparent in the way that Joyce lived her life that she received her power from the Holy Spirit. She let her thoughts be those of a conqueror in Christ, and so she was a conqueror in Christ. I have never seen a power like it before. It is unbreakable, unshakeable, incorruptible, indestructible, everlasting, and now, even with her body physically gone, her power still overcomes me. I can see Joyce's influence all around me. I can see it in the hospitals that she spent so much time in, I can see it in the friends and family she left behind, I can see it on the very ground she once walked on. Perhaps the most apparent place where I see Joyce's spirit is in her friend, Norma. I am and forever will be haunted by the hope Norma still possesses despite all that I have thrown at her. If there's one thing I am sure of, it is this: God is bigger than all things, even me, Cancer.

Afterword

I never got a chance to meet Joyce Carrell before she left this world to be with Jesus, but the information I was given to write her story gave me insight into the incredible woman I know she was and is. If there's one thing I learned from Joyce through this process, it's that we should live life like we're living. It sounds simple, but too often, we are told to "live like we're dying." Joyce was living proof of how blessed life on this earth can be when we live it with the mentality that Jesus saved us from death when he died on the cross in our place. They say "you can learn a lot about a person by what their friends say about them", and based on the beautiful eulogy Carol sent me and the incredible story Norma sent me, I would say Joyce was a pretty amazing, strong, and God fearing woman. Thank you for reading, I hope you can learn from Joyce as much as I did. I look forward to meeting her in heaven one day.

In Him,

Libby A Kirkpatrick, Editor

Beauty From Ashes

Robin Raney

Pappy made her a beautiful rocking horse for her second birthday. Pal's mane was big and fluffy, his wooden coat shined and he was ready to play. Katie's eyes sparkled as she rocked and sang, "Jesus loves me, this I know." Our beautiful two-year-old was not normally this expressive, and we had never heard her spontaneously burst into song.

I teared up and leaned back on my husband, Don. After the many challenges, scares, surgeries and health crisis of the past two years, it was precious to see that Katie's joy pointed her towards Jesus. She was Daddy's girl and Mommy's angel, full of energy and light. We delighted in our happy, sweet girl with strawberry blond curls and sparkly big blue eyes. But at the same time we were dealing with scary ideas like "developmental delays," "failure to thrive," and "possible brain damage." Doctors were shaking their heads, running hands over her shining curls and saying, "We'll know more later."

As we waited, I prayed, mediated over God's Word, squared my shoulders, picked up my fearless mommy sword and determined that I would do everything in my power to love and protect Katie while finding every possible resource to bring out the best in this beautiful child. We continued to be bombarded:

"I'm sorry, but your daughter is not well-behaved enough to join the toddler's ballet class."

"We are not going to promote your daughter into the Pre-K class. She is just not ready. She doesn't even know her colors and shapes, and is still not potty trained."

"I know your husband is a full-time student, but have you considered that Katie might be better behaved if you quit work and stayed home with her full time?"

"There just isn't a place for Katie for Vacation Bible School. If you are not able to stay with her, would you please come pick her up?"

Our hearts were ready for a second baby. My women's bible study group had several women who were grieving over miscarriages and waiting, along with me, for another child to join our families. We talked about Mother's Day and how hard it was going to be this year and several said they planned to stand in the back of the sanctuary and cry. I was asked to sing a special song for the Mother's Day service. *Lord, after the pain of two miscarriages, how can I sing when my heart is so sad and my arms still do not have another baby? I will trust you. I know you have a plan.*

Stephen, a little boy in Katie's Sunday School class, asked for prayer that God would give him a little sister. *How sweet,* I thought, *Katie is asking God to give us a baby, too.* On Mother's Day, as I stepped onto the podium, Stephen's family stood up with a newborn nestled in a pink blanket, offering praise for the adoption of their daughter. Peace washed over me, *I can trust the Lord to put families together in His way, for His glory and according to His purpose.* Six weeks later, we were overjoyed to learn that we were expecting!

The date was set for the arrival of our long awaited second child. For the past six years, I had enjoyed an upwardly mobile career with a luxury retail powerhouse that shared many similarities to the movie, *The Devil Wears Prada.* While the days were long and the job could be stressful, our financial needs were met and we had great healthcare. This gave our family an unusual amount of security while Don was working on his Master's degree. Long work days with an hour commute each way, juggling Katie's various medical needs and many doctor's appointments had taken its toll and I was on bed-rest with pre-eclampsia. Now almost four, Katie was still not sleeping through the night, not potty trained, and her vocabulary was not keeping pace with her frustrations for a world that seemed to be slowly passing her by. There were no play dates, no little friends, no ballet lessons or soccer team, no birthday party invitations— just me, Don and Katie. The world seemed to hold us at a distance, not understanding Katie's unusual dance through life. Our parents were very supportive, yet they were twelve hours away. Too far away for spontaneous dinners, date nights for Don and I, or help with a sick baby. They were, however, very creative in how they spent time with us and in building relationships with their grandchildren, and visited at every opportunity.

Two days before labor was to be induced, I stood in the shower crying out to the Lord. *Thank you so much for this precious baby that is about to arrive—you alone know how much I want this new little life. How am I going to do this Lord? Don is still in graduate school. We only pass each other when I get home from work and he leaves for his night job. My work hours are long and Katie's needs are high. How am I going to continue working, supporting, cleaning, washing, ironing while caring for Katie plus a newborn? How?*

Once again, a precious peace washed over me as I was reminded of Stephen and his new, adopted baby sister and my God who builds and restores. *Robin, you can trust me with your family. I heard your prayers and have sent a precious little soul that will fit perfectly into your family and bring tremendous joy!* Joseph was born two days later, nearly nine months to the day that Stephen's little sister was introduced on Mother's Day. Joseph was a healthy, strong and happy baby who seamlessly fit right into our little family.

Katie and Joseph both attended the childcare development center at the seminary, a bright and cheerful facility that was overseen by an expert in early childhood development. At her prompting, we asked our school district to evaluate Katie's readiness for kindergarten. At the first evaluation, the diagnostic team watched Katie race around the table with curls flying and dismissed all of our concerns as ADHD.

"No! There's more; you have to keep looking," I said as I captured my flying wild child and held her in my arms. They finally agreed to expand their evaluation. After a two and a half year journey to find a diagnosis and get assistance with the mysteries surrounding Katie, the big day arrived. I should have been tipped off, by the big box of Kleenex placed in front of me, as I faced the developmental evaluation committee. I heard a scary and not yet common word, **Autism.**

The special education teacher reached over and patted my hand, "You may have people tell you that autistic children are a result of cold and uncaring mothers – we know that is not true, so don't you believe it for a minute."

Was I cold and uncaring or just detached? Of course that was not true! I fought for Katie at every turn. They did share that not many children had autism, about 1 in 10,000. To be fair, they probably did not have any idea of how to deal with an autistic child. So they sent me home without manuals, brochures, referrals, suggestions or instructions. They just smiled and waved saying, "We'll see Katie in kindergarten next year! Good luck!"

The very next week, I was able to attend a seminar on autism by a leading international expert and began to immerse myself in the study of this mysterious disorder. We have a starting point, I thought to myself. We will get a second opinion, read everything we can get our hands on, find the right doctors, start therapy. We can mobilize! While it was a relief to finally have a diagnosis, it was terrifying to learn that this was a diagnosis that would last a lifetime. According to the Center for Disease Control:

Autism Spectrum Disorder (ASD) is a developmental disability that can cause significant social, communication and behavioral challenges. There is often nothing about how a person with ASD looks that sets them apart from other people, but people with ASD may communicate, interact, behave and learn in ways that are different from most other people. The learning, thinking and problem-solving abilities of people with ASD can range from gifted to severely challenged.

While I was barreling through life looking for solutions, I was also grieving. In fact, the more I learned, the more I grieved. I cried all the way through my lengthy commute each morning, repaired my make-up in my car, put on a "happy face," walked into the office and lost myself in work until it was time to cry all the way home in the evenings, wipe away the tears again, and walked into our little dollhouse ready to love my little family to pieces and conquer autism. Night and weekends were filled with my own versions of play therapy. *Thank you Lord. Now that we have a diagnosis, we can conquer this, right?*

Don was now working on his doctorate and teaching Master's level classes, Joseph was crawling, rolling and growing and Katie was still a beautiful little, irrepressible mystery. I still picked up my mommy sword daily, cried to the Lord and fought for Katie. I still remember the "meet the teacher" night a few days before kindergarten. Katie refused to separate from me and would only remain in her assigned chair if I sat on the floor right next to her. I saw the looks coming from other parents, the "Have you not been teaching your daughter ANYTHING?" look. Their expressions were a lot like of the "What kind of mother are you?" glare that I frequently encountered. Within the first six weeks, we were receiving special services from the school to provide additional support for Katie. By the end of her kindergarten year, Katie was less verbal and more frustrated. I asked the school district to let her repeat kindergarten. Instead, they insisted on moving her to a self-contained classroom where Katie would only spend 30 minutes a day in a general education classroom and would have more help "learning the rules of school." I felt we were moving backwards instead of forward.

My vision for Katie included a wagon train of support with doctors, therapists, knowledgeable and supportive teachers, and a beautiful happy ending. I worked tirelessly towards that end. Other parents of special needs children thanked me for being a trailblazer and challenging our school district to provide appropriate services for our children. While others may have viewed me as strong and brave, it wasn't unusual for me to be sitting on the floor of our bathroom at 3:30 a.m. reading my bible. I was crying to the Lord for strength, claiming, "A dimly burning wick He will not extinguish, and a bruised reed He will not break." I begged, "Lord, please give me the strength for another day." As my alarm clock would sound in the mornings, I would wake up crying, ignore the exhaustion, and brace myself for another frustrating morning of guiding Katie through her morning routine and a long day at work.

It shames me to admit, but I was a self-righteous mother who believed that many children who took medication for behavioral issues were being medicated for their parents' convenience. I had brushed away suggestions from medical professionals that Katie might benefit from medication. One night, when Katie was six, we were singing goodnight songs and snuggling on her bed at bedtime. Putting Katie to bed had always been a challenge, and I was accustomed to a lengthy, nightly ritual. This night, Katie was frenzied. Taking her favorite doll, Tammie, she slammed her into my face, compressing my cornea. The next morning, God gave me the grace to realize that Katie was trying to get my attention and she needed help. It was time to put aside my bias, take our pediatrician's advice, and make our first appointment with a pediatric psychiatrist. Prescriptions in hand, I asked the pharmacist to review the medications with me. One, she said, was a classic ADHD medication and the other was an anti-psychotic medication used to treat schizophrenia. Tears overflowing, I stepped out in faith and filled the prescriptions, as I prayed for peace in our family and help for Katie.

It should have been the happiest of days when Don graduated with his PhD. As he left early for the ceremony, I looked at him as he left the house for graduation and said, "I don't even know you anymore and I'm not sure I even like you." I cringe even now as I remember those hurtful, yet heartfelt words. Nine years of Don's full-time graduate and post-graduate work while he worked part-time had taken its' toll on our marriage. My hopes were high that this would be the year that Don started working full-time in his field. The pictures from that day show a beautiful family dressed for a celebration. A few months later, as the last door closed on a full-time professorship for the upcoming school year, I felt my carefully coiffed exterior begin to crumble as the dark, depressed places in my mind and heart began to expand.

Now in the third grade, Katie spent her entire school day with other autistic students, many of whom were non-verbal and some were prone to explosive outbursts. While she was considered "high functioning", the school still felt that her behavior prevented her from being able to function in a "regular" classroom. I was convinced that if we could discover how Katie learned and processed information, we would find new opportunities to help her move forward, but was unable to gain support for my ideas.

The same precious special education teacher who patted my hand when Katie was diagnosed at four and a half had now directed Katie's lesson plans for four years. When a freak accident took her life, our champion, Katie's fearless protector and my guide through this confusing and unpredictable maze of autism was gone. Our special education community had lost its' pied piper. The students were lost and confused, the teachers' aides were crying, and this little self-contained classroom that was Katie's entire social realm was in chaos. Katie was in crisis and began biting herself and engaging in other self-destructive behaviors. The simplest of questions, such as, "Would you rather have a peanut butter and jelly sandwich or a turkey sandwich?" could send her spiraling out of control and derail family plans for hours.

Four years after a diagnosis, instead of showing improvement, Katie was digressing. At the end of her third grade year, Katie could not read the simplest of books, was becoming less verbal and I was in a battle with the school district, pushing for services and solutions. Katie's days were still full of finger painting and having an aide read the same stories over and over to her instead of helping her read for herself. I wanted her retained in the third grade, in a regular education classroom with a full-time aid. Once again, the school disagreed. Many battle scars later, at age nine, Katie began her first year as a full-time regular education student with a full-time aide. She was more than two years behind academically, read at a kindergarten level and was so frustrated, she made no attempt to participate in class.

It hurts to admit that I once mocked in my heart another special needs mother when she told me that I was the only parent she knew who wasn't on medication. I prided myself in hiding my depression, thinking that my power suit, smile, high heels and a beautiful little house with a smiling family would keep my secret of depression safe. Regardless of my determination to plow through, I was not invincible.

Each time my doctor discussed depression and suggested medication for me, I felt it would be a sign of spiritual weakness to take the "simple route" instead of building my faith and dependence on the Lord. Of course, the Lord would sustain me; my love for Katie would conquer all.

When Katie was in the fourth grade, one of her pre-school teachers from the seminary reached out and asked if she could begin babysitting for us. With no immediate family in the area, the idea of a date night was foreign to us and our marriage had suffered. Still working long hours, I felt tremendous guilt taking any additional time away from Katie and Joseph, and often resented leaving the children to spend time with Don. This marked the first of many changes in our home and the beginning of a new spark in our marriage. Don began taking Katie to Therapeutic Horseback Riding one night each week, freeing me to have a play date with Joseph. We worked, played, worshipped and tried to live a "normal life" while developmental milestone after milestone passed us by.

We had still not been successful in teaching Katie to swim, ride a bike, cross the street, read a book by herself or even get herself dressed. I still bathed her, brushed her hair, washed her face and brushed her teeth. Autism was a giant that I could not conquer or fix: I felt like a complete failure.

Still commuting over an hour each way to work, I sometimes hoped that an 18-wheeler would run over me and take my life. Of course, I would never choose to leave my beautiful and precious children, but if the Lord in His infinite wisdom chose to take me home to Him, that would be okay. Don was still not working in his field and was deeply discouraged. My depression was now affecting my mental clarity and I began making mistakes at work. My job, the one place where I felt successful and the source of financial stability for my family, was soon going to be placed on the altar.

Driving to work one morning, sobbing with exhaustion and discouragement, I felt a presence in my spirit say, *You do not have because you do not ask - tell me what you want; tell me what you need. Call to me and I will answer you.* I poured my heart out and asked for a way of escape. I prayed that God would find a way for me to leave my job and focus on my family and health. Later that day, a senior human resources officer called me to his office, reviewed my successful twelve-year history with the company, commented that I was not at my best and was under-performing, and asked how he could help. "Tell me what you want, tell me what you need." I could not believe that he was echoing the conversation I had with the Lord that very morning! By grace, I resigned with a generous package and went home to my family.

Now in the darkest days of depression, I was diagnosed with "Situational Depression", began taking medicine, and seeing a counselor. A friend from church prayed for me from Isaiah 43:2-3:

When you pass through the waters, I will be with you; and through the rivers, they will not overflow you.

When you walk through the fire, you will not be scorched, nor will the flame burn you.

For I am the Lord your God, the Holy One of Israel, your Savior. (NAS)

As I meditated on this passage, and many passages attributed to David from the Book of Psalms, I gained confidence that depression would not defeat me, but my Lord would strengthen and sustain me.

Being the self-sufficient, strong willed, choleric workaholic that I am, I rested and recuperated for a blink and soon accepted a job closer to home with less pay and less responsibility. I ignored the doctor's counsel that he did not feel I was ready to return to work. It did not take long for me to be fired from my new job and the job after that. I was in a fog and was no longer able to escape from the difficulties at home by pouring my full concentration into work. Don was also out of work and I felt that my career was over. With God's amazing provision we were humbled yet sustained. Through God's grace we paid every bill on time. We had been a part of the same Sunday School class for many years, and the love from these couples overflowed as they walked alongside us. Our pastor asked for my help with a project at church, allowing me to use gifts I didn't know I had that would come into play in future jobs.

PhD in hand, Don had applied for four years to universities to teach theology and had received feedback that he needed pastoral experience before equipping others for the pastorate. In the meantime, he was working jobs outside of his field, including working part-time for FedEx. I was mad at God. Had I not been faithful to support Don through two years of missionary service and nine years of graduate school and then another four years of applying for teaching jobs? Had I not supported our family financially working VERY HARD, even at the expense of my emotional health, while Don prepared for a career in academia? Why was his career not moving forward? Had we missed the will of God? Friend after friend asked me if there were some hidden sin in our life that kept our family from thriving. We were "wandering in the wilderness" as I refused to follow Don into the pastorate. After all, I reasoned, Don promised me when we were dating that he would never pastor and I had NEVER seen an introverted pastor – did one even exist? I did not play the piano and was not the "Wear beige and keep your mouth shut" kind of girl, so why would God ask me to be a pastor's wife? This could not possibly be God's will for our lives - either Don missed God's will when he asked me to be his wife or he was missing God's will now. I learned in this season of anger and resentment that God wants us to bring our hearts to — good, bad and ugly. Just lay it all out there and stand before our Lord in total transparency. He is big enough to handle it all. He already knows your heart and He wants you to give it all to Him.

1 Peter 5: 6-7 changed my angry, rebellious heart and I committed to follow Don. With immeasurable support

from our pastor and home church, we finally agreed that the next time God opened a door, we were walking through it.

God really has a sense of humor. I never saw myself as a pastor's wife. In fact, I broke up with three boys who felt called to the ministry. In an interview with a church search committee, I was asked if I planned to work.

"Only if I want to send my children to college and be able to retire someday", I quipped. *Did I want to work? Of course! I thrived on the sense of accomplishment of a job well done and the opportunity to productively escape from the stress of parenting a special needs child.*

"Well", they said, "There is a Dairy Queen, a barbeque place and a bank nearby and *that's* about it." Not only were we considering a move to a very small town, the church was two hours west, so we would now be 14 hours away from our parents.

Stepping out in faith, Don accepted the position, knowing that we could not meet our financial obligations on the salary provided by the small church. We put our house on the market and moved from my 2,000 sq. ft. dream home into a 1,200 sq. ft. 25-year-old double wide trailer – our first parsonage. The sale of our home was affected by an overabundance of homes on the market and we were soon taking out cash advances against credit cards to cover the house payment. The "Big City Girl" who had never lived in a small town now lived next door to the little white church where Don served without any neighbors nearby. It was a 15 minute drive just to take the children to their bus stop and another 20 minute ride on the school bus just to get to town!

Moving only two hours away meant that Katie could keep the same developmental pediatrician, child psychiatrist, caseworkers and other healthcare professionals. The wagon train that supported Katie would not be completely disturbed. Don's new health insurance declined to insure Katie and me, so we found ourselves paying for her medications and healthcare out of pocket, often by credit card. I discontinued my medication "cold turkey" and prayed for a job with benefits and a salary that would bridge the gap between Don's salary and our obligations.

My undergraduate degrees were in Accounting and Business Administration with my entire career focused on retail management, buying and analysis. I dreamed of a career where I worked with people and programs, making my community a better place to live. I wanted to use my financial background but did not want profitability to dictate every decision. I wanted to make a difference in the world, not just help make it all pretty.

Don's first day on the job, a church member took him to lunch with his service club. During announcements, a woman shared that she was leaving her job and a replacement had not been found. Don called me after lunch. "You know how you always dreamed about a job outside of retail, but didn't know what to call it," he asked? "Well I found it, and I'm faxing you the job description and application."

Much to my delight, I was offered a position as the director of a chamber of commerce. When God called Don to pastor, He prepared a place for each of us. Katie and Joseph were settled in school, Don was enjoying his place of service and I loved my new role in non-profit management.

Katie's thirteenth birthday arrived, and I grieved as Katie seemed to have resigned herself to a life of having others attend to her needs. While other young teens were meeting for the movies and going to school dances, Katie was at home playing with her barbies. Her birthday was celebrated with an adult couple from our church, not with other tweens.

I shared my concerns with our developmental pediatrician that Katie seemed to have stopped developing mentally and socially. As naive as it sounds, I assumed if Katie was four years behind developmentally at 13, then at 18 she would seem to be 14, and by 25 she would be as ready for the world as any 21 year old! With a shadow of sorrow in her eyes, the kind doctor took my hand and explained that many teens with developmental delays simply stop progressing and remain in the same developmental stage for the rest of their lives. In addition, what I thought were simply outbursts due to teenage hormones might be pointing to a mood disorder (a less scary word than bipolar). The idea that Katie may have stopped developing was terrifying and sent me to my knees, begging the Lord for more time to grow. *Lord, I don't know how much more I can take.* More medication, more "Let's wait and see," and more grieving.

Don's next pastorate moved us four hours further west to a tiny town of less than 1,000 and 18 hours from our parents. This move also provided an opportunity for Don to teach as an adjunct professor at a nearby university. While Katie's wagon train of support had be re-built from scratch, we quickly learned that we were just outside the largest medical community between Dallas and Los Angeles, and Katie would have excellent care. With Katie and Joseph settled in school and Don busy with his new responsibilities, I accepted a new position leading a mid-size non-profit.

Katie was our little school's first student with autism. Much to our delight, the precious special education teacher loved Katie and Katie loved her. In two short years, Katie was testing on grade level for the very first time! While she was treated with kindness, she was also very protected and isolated. I accompanied Katie on her senior trip to Disney World with her classmates and had the life changing experience of walking a mile or two in Katie's shoes. Classmates offered to carry her luggage (which she could do), but no one sat down to have a meal with us or invited her to join them on a ride or to watch the fireworks. The school staff made sure we entered the gates to the Magic Kingdom and met them at the end of the day to return to the hotel, but we were completely alone the rest of the time. How could this be? Katie had been in school with these teachers and students for five years. Was she always so alone? While she was never invited to the movies or to attend a school event with other students, I had no idea how isolated she was on a daily basis. As her classmates made plans for life after high school, I was pleading with God to show us the next step for Katie, and begging Him that she might continue to grow and advance. He had always provided a place for all four of us as we followed Don in his ministry, so I believed with all my heart that there was a place for Katie in the next season of her life. I just couldn't image what was next and prayed earnestly that God would show us a future and a hope for Katie (Jeremiah 29:11). Many students with Autism finish high school and become so discouraged in their work or academic endeavors that they end up living a very lonely life, sleeping, eating and playing video games.

Much to our delight, Katie was accepted into the Transition Academy of the Burkhart Center for Autism Education & Research at Texas Tech University. This private academy is a one-of-a-kind university affiliated program designed to help high school graduates with autism prepare for higher education or the workforce by focusing on life skills, social skills and job skills. My office was just a few blocks from campus and Katie was excited about commuting with me. Katie told me she no longer felt "invisible" and explained that she always felt that people just ignored and overlooked her because they didn't understand her. My heart broke and rejoiced at the same time. God had provided the perfect place for Katie and she was growing and thriving!

I developed a passion for helping Katie and others like her find their place in the world. The Center for Disease Control announced in 2014 that autism now affects 1 in 68 children - a huge difference from the 1 in 10,000 when Katie was diagnosed in 1998. Challenges associated with autism present a growing healthcare challenge and emerging workforce crisis. Much like I was driven to develop resources for Katie, I wanted to be part of finding solutions for a growing population of adults in the Autism Spectrum.

My Savior, Lord, Shield and Protector provided the perfect place where my faith, family, passion for autism awareness, retail and non-profit background all combined into a single mission: I became the CEO of Goodwill Industries of Northwest Texas. I am passionate about the Goodwill mission of helping people remove barriers to employment. This amazing social enterprise recognizes abilities, not disabilities, and is a preferred employer for people with disabilities. One of my first actions was to form an official partnership between Goodwill and the Burkhart Center Transition Academy. Our staff developed a training class to teach students to write their resumes, learn how to search for jobs and practice their interview skills. After completing this training, students were given the opportunity to interview for paid internships at Goodwill. Transition Academy students are accompanied by a job coach who helps them develop their work skills and social skills. After the first semester, the Transition Academy asked us to develop and lead customer service training for the students, and we did. It is pure joy to watch Katie and her peers at work each day. Our entire organization benefits when we seek the specials skills and interests of each employee and give them the tools to succeed and thrive. I'm proud to say that Katie was my inspiration for joining Goodwill.

What about my depression? Eleven years ago, I was deeply depressed. My marriage and career were in chaos and I was merely shuffling through each day, managing the basic necessities of life and parenting. When my mother told me my eyes were flat and lifeless and had "lost their sparkle," I finally began to seek solutions.

I'm a fairly private person, so it is a big leap for me to publically share my journey with depression but is an important part of our journey with autism. The reality of a lifetime diagnosis for your child, along the companionship of pain, frustration and grief makes me wonder if depression might be common in special needs families. My motivation is simply to encourage mothers of special needs children, and to share a story of hope and victory.

According to the Centers for Disease Control and Prevention, about nine percent of adult Americans have feelings of depression. In recent years, God has opened a few doors for me to offer encouragement to others who were struggling with depression. Don and I know my personal warning signs and I have a short list of action steps to take when I feel depressed. After working with my doctor to find the right kind of medication for me, I have not had a major episode in ten years and understand that depression is not a sign of weakness or lack of faith. While the circumstances that initiated my diagnosis of Situational Depression have not changed, my response to the circumstances and the way I support my emotional well being, have.

If any reader has questions or feels she may be depressed, I encourage them to see their doctor. Depression hurts and affects not only the one who is suffering, but the entire family. Life is too amazing to miss out on anything from not feeling your best!

When Don began his Master's program, the seminary cautioned married students to nurture their marriage, explaining that the divorce rate for Master's level students was one out of every three couples. When Don began his doctorate, the seminary quoted a divorce rate of 68% for post-graduate students. We learned, after Katie's diagnosis, that the divorce rate for parents of special needs children was 86%. I don't know where these statistics came from, but they certainly got our attention.

Don and I recently returned from an Alaskan cruise to celebrate our 25th wedding anniversary. Looking back to the days when I resented leaving Katie and Joseph with a babysitter to go on a date, I'm grateful we made time to be alone to remind ourselves that we were called first to be a couple and then to be parents. Young mothers, nurturing your marriage is a gift to your children; respecting your husband is a gift to your marriage. Don and I are grateful for our healthy, happy, growing marriage and look forward to continuing to walk together in the Lord.

Recently, Katie asked a friend from school to spend the night at our house. It was pure joy to see Katie and her friend giggling and talking, eating pizza while joking around with Joseph and one of his friends. Her first friend, how precious! A few weeks later, another friend came to spend the night. At twenty, Katie's eyes are bright and sparkling again and she is happy to tell others about her school and her job. She is excited to be learning new things and is making strides towards becoming more independent.

Acquaintances often ask me if Katie will always live with us and what her future holds. Will she marry? Will she have children? Live independently? Drive? Attend college? With a smile and a much lighter heart, I say, "I don't know. Katie is still growing and developing. The Lord provides and isn't finished with us. We'll see what He has in store for Katie!"

Reflections on what I learned on this journey...

God creates each of us in His own image and forms us to His delight. (Genesis 1:27, Isaiah 43:7, Isaiah 44:2, Matthew 10:30, Luke 12:7, Jeremiah 1:5,)

Our strength comes from the Lord and when He calls us to a task, He equips us as well. (Isaiah 40: 31, Psalms 139: 1-24, Galatians 6:9, Hebrews 13:21)

He can make beauty from ashes, transform our mourning and turn a spirit of weariness into a mantle of praise. (Isaiah 61: 1-3, Matthew 11: 28-30, Hebrews 12:3)

Marriage, by design, was created to endure. (Ecclesiastes 4:12, Malachi 2: 14-16, Matthew 5: 31-32, Matthew 19: 1-30). We are given instruction on how to live together (I Corinthians 13: 4-7, Ephesians 5: 25, Ephesians 5:33, I Peter 3: 1-11) this lasting marriage relationship is beloved of God, designed to sharpen and challenge us in our daily lives. (Isaiah 62:5, Proverbs 27:17, Mark 10: 2-12)

God has a unique plan for each of us – ALL of us. (Jeremiah 29:11, I Peter 4:10)

God's Word is enduring and sustaining and will strengthen and equip us: All scripture is inspired by God and profitable for teaching, for reproof, for correction, for training in righteousness that the man of God may be adequate, equipped for every good work. (2 Timothy, 3: 16,17)

About the Author

Robin Raney is a graduate of Birmingham-Southern College in Birmingham, Alabama where she earned bachelor's degrees in accounting and business administration. She is also a graduate of the Institute of Organizational Management. Robin and her husband, Don, met when she visited his home church 27 years ago. Don is a pastor and professor with a special interest in Kenya missions. Married for 25 years, their fast-paced family includes children Katie and Joseph, and Shih Tzu, Bear. Their family's journey with Autism began in 1998 when Katie was diagnosed at age four. Robin is an advocate for Autism Awareness and serves on an Advisory Board for the Texas Tech University Burkhart Center for Autism Education and Awareness.

Prior to taking the helm as CEO of Goodwill Industries of Northwest Texas, Raney served as the Vice-President of Business Development for the Lubbock Texas Chamber of Commerce, CEO of the American Red Cross South Plains Regional Chapter in Lubbock, Texas and Executive Director for the Graham Chamber of Commerce, located in Graham, Texas. Before beginning her career in non-profit management, Robin enjoyed a twenty year career in retail buying, analysis and management. In her spare time, she enjoys retail, spa and music therapy.

He Gives and Takes Away

Jana Shelburne - Brown

I am Jana.

I was born Jana Hodges on July 11, 1962.

I became Jana Shelburne on December 30, 1983.

Yet again on March 13, 2010 I was renamed, Jana Shelburne-Brown.

I have lived and loved.

I have lived and lost.

I have lived through grief. However, I have <u>not</u> grieved like those who have no hope. 1 Thessalonians 4:13

I am a daughter of the One who gives and takes away.

I am a child of the One who gives again.

This is my story of HOPE.

I was 25 years old and had been married to my wonderful husband, David, for four years. We were living in Mid-West City, Oklahoma where David grew up. He was working as a Youth Minister at a church there. We had a darling son, Ryan, who was two years old and were eagerly awaiting the arrival of our next little one. Life was moving right along.

On March 25, 1988 my first baby girl was born. I was in the surgical delivery room for my second C-section. David was not allowed into the room when Lindsey was born, though I don't remember why. The two doctors were just talking away until Lindsey's leg presented itself, and then the next thing I heard was, "Doctor there are only two lines." They were referring to her umbilical cord. Normal ones have three "lines" of arteries and veins to insure nutrients and oxygen for the baby while in-utero. All of a sudden it became really quiet. You can be sure that there's reason for concern when a room of medical personnel gets really quiet. The next thing I heard was the Apgar score. Hers was only a 3 out of a perfect 10. They allowed me to look at her very briefly, and then they took her to the NICU.

They took me into recovery but were unable to locate David. Soon a doctor came in to talk to me about Lindsey's condition. This conversation happened while I was alone. (This situation of my being alone while terrible medical news is delivered will repeat itself in years to come.) He told me that because of the malformation of the cord, she hadn't received proper nourishment and was not doing well. There were numerous things they were worried about, so they decided to take her to Children's Hospital in Oklahoma City, which was around 30 minutes away. Our lives were forever changed.

Soon after the doctor told me the news, David and his mom came in and were so excited to have seen her through the nursery window. They had no idea what is happening! Well, I just burst into tears and told them to go find a doctor. Two hours after delivery, they had prepared her for transport and attempted to put me in a wheel chair so I could see her before she left. I promptly passed-out! I did get to see her for a minute, but had to remain there to recover, and she had to go where she would receive the care she needed. Poor David was torn between being with me and being with Lindsey at the other hospital. It was a crazy, hectic few days!

Then we began finding out so many different things that were wrong with Lindsey. She was neither breathing nor eating well. I had been pumping breast milk while separated from her, but the nurses hadn't been giving it to her because she looked so much like a fetal-alcohol syndrome baby. They assumed I was an alcoholic because of the way Lindsey looked, and that my milk would not be good. When I finally arrived at the NICU and the nurses got to know me, they immediately began giving my milk to not only Lindsey but also to other infants.

So many medical tests. There were just so many things wrong with Lindsey from top to bottom. She was missing the connective tissue that joins the two sides of her brain that lets the left and right sides of the brain talk to each other. The right lobe of her brain was not fully developed. She had a very, very high palate. It was not quite cleft, but caused feeding issues. Her eyes had difficulty tracking and focusing. She had several things going on with her heart, some of which actually cleared up over time. One kidney was out of place, the other one did not fully function, but the two together functioned as one kidney.

One of my most vivid memories is the doctors wanting to do a medical test with radioactive material to see how Lindsey's digestive system was working. She was beginning to be a "failure to thrive" baby because she just wasn't gaining weight. So, they walked in with their big rubber suits and their box with a big radioactive materials sign. As they proceeded to pull out a big needle out of that protective foam lined box I thought, "You're wanting to put that into my baby? Wow!"

We took her home after six weeks in the NICU. We were told that she may not see, she may not hear, but she is stable, so take her home. Scary! She had two different stomach surgeries within the first few months and was left with a feeding tube. Breathing complications developed into bouts with pneumonia, which brought on a tracheotomy tube. There was also oxygen to be administered as well as the heart monitor to watch.

We all hated to leave Lindsay in the hospital with the uncertainty of her very survival but knew we had another child to worry about. During Lindsey's stays in the hospital ICU, we would make sure that one parent was home with two-year-old Ryan in the evenings. He stayed with a woman who had an in-home daycare and a sister-in-law during the days. He was such a stout little toddler, generally seen with a baby-doll under one arm. He carried that baby around like a football, because he wanted his baby sister to be with him. He loved counting her fingers and toes and always commented on her various boo-boos. Oddly enough, he was also quick to comment on the developmental milestones of other babies. He had no idea that his sister's experience wasn't normal.

Lindsey's medical bills were very high. We were paying $700 a month for health insurance, grateful to have the help with the mounting costs. Lindsey was born in 1988 when AIDs was becoming a full-blown epidemic. Because of the resulting increased medical costs, many mom and pop insurance providers were forced to close.

Of course, we had purchased our health insurance from a small local provider who went under. So for a time we had no insurance coverage for Lindsey.

During our fight against the Oklahoma Insurance Commission, at around six months into Lindsey's life, David lost his job. We decided to move to Lubbock, where my parents lived. Let me tell you that a six-hour car ride with a medically critical six month old and a toddler is no easy undertaking! We moved in with my parents, which was not ideal but we had little choice. With this move, we had to re-establish doctors and medical care.

For the next months we dealt with persistent illnesses—pneumonia was a constant companion. At six months Lindsey only still weighed about nine pounds. She was very tiny and frail looking, with an ashen coloring. One positive change was putting Lindsey on a feeding pump, which was a slow, continuous feed through her tube. This allowed her weight to double within three months. After a time on the feeding pump, her appearance dramatically improved. Her coloring was all sweet and pink! She just looked so much more "alive." We knew at this point that she could both see and hear.

Lindsey spent seven of the first thirteen months of her life in the hospital. Every little thing ended up in at least a ten-day stay. If she was in ICU, we could leave her and come home for the night. If she was in a regular room, either David or I had to stay. She simply could not be left alone for any length of time.

We never had a name for what was wrong with Lindsey. Her ultimate diagnosis became "multiple congenital anomalies." In other words, "We are just going to treat her symptoms, but have no diagnosis for you." It turns out that with as many diseases that the medical experts can name, there are just as many diseases that remain a mystery to them. Most likely, something happened in the first 8-12 weeks of my pregnancy while Lindsey's cells were dividing. It could have been something as simple as my having a cold or the flu, which caused her problems.

This was my big lesson—I don't always have to know the answer. I just have to be able to deal with what has been placed in front of me. Having the answer doesn't necessarily change what I'm going to have to do anyway. This was such an important lesson for me to learn at this time. Lindsey was just unique, and we loved her.

After Lindsey turned one, she qualified for a special home nursing program for chronically ill children. She really needed the level of care that a nursing home could provide, but we wanted her home with us. Instead, we received the training and learned how to take care of her ourselves. I regularly changed her trach tube and suctioned her airway every hour or so. My shift lasted until 4 a.m. So I could sleep, David took care of her until around 8:00 when he went to work in the morning. You can imaging the level of exhaustion! David and I did medical procedures for her that many nurses don't regularly do.

Lindsey still had no health insurance, but qualified for Social Security Disability. In order for her to qualify for Medicaid, we had to keep our annual income below $17,000 for a family of four. That was low for even back then!

We lived a very isolated life. David and I took turns going to church and Bible classes with Ryan. Every time we tried to take her to a church activity, she would get sick. So, we just took turns so Lindsey could stay home.

I credit the nursing help we received in our home for saving our family. We basically had a mini-ICU in our dining room. That way I could see Lindsey, Ryan could interact with her, and we could carry on with the rest of the household activities.

The stress was overwhelming. I recognized I had reached my breaking point. With the nurse there, I was finally able to tell David, "I've got to go. If I don't go now, there's not going to be anything left of me." He travelled with his job, so at times, it was just me...taking care of everything.

He asked me before I left for my trip, "What do you think? Are we going to be taking separate vacations for the rest of our lives?"

My response was, "I don't know about that. All I know is that for right now, I have to go."

So, I took our foreign exchange student (we had a student living with us—he had lost his place to live, so we offered him a place) and 3-year-old Ryan and went to my sister's place at the beach. Beaches are my haven, my calming, renewing place. I took the one and only car we had and was gone for a week. After that break, I was ready to continue on, refreshed and renewed.

That was such a pivotal moment in our marriage. David was really able to experience what I dealt with on a daily basis. The level of care that Lindsey required was a full-time job in itself. In turn I was able to appreciate how hard he worked to provide financially for the family so I could stay home. He learned that week just how much I did all day, every day. He had a great deal of respect for what my responsibilities entailed. We were only 26 years old. It was such a huge learning curve for us. We each had our own roles and had learned to appreciate them.

When Lindsey was two, she was able to have the trach removed. We tried to take her off of the oxygen as well, but she still needed it because of scarred lungs from many bouts with pneumonia. I learned how to use liquid oxygen so I could fill her tanks myself. With this change we were able to take her on trips. Traveling around with a tank of liquid oxygen in the back of our van was really not the wisest thing to do, but we didn't let it stop us from living life. We tried to live as normal a family life as possible. Once we took Lindsey up to the New Mexico mountains with the extended family. We even made it all the way to Houston (over 500 miles) to visit family. Lindsey ended up in the hospital that trip, but that was just normal for us.

After her second year, her health became more and more stable and she would only need hospitalization every 2-3 months. We were able to do many different kinds of therapies and groundbreaking programs. Lindsey was an innovator and really paved the way for other children. She was the first one in our county to be on this nursing program. She was the first one in the county to be transported to school, by bus, with an oxygen tank. She was the first child in our area to get a specialized wheelchair. It had a collapsible, beanbag type of seating that completely conformed to her body and gave her the support she needed to sit up. They are common now, but she was the first. We were able to do a lot of innovative things because we had such great people in place to help us. God always placed just who we needed in our lives. For example, a place called Parenting Cottage helped us with occupational therapies to help us see how far she could progress.

The nurse we had was really special. We actually met her while she was working at the hospital. I noticed that she would always go the extra mile, so we offered her the job of helping us take care of Lindsey at home. Having her there gave me the freedom to take naps, to go to lunch with my husband, all kinds of things that I'd never be able to do without her.

Lindsey was doing well. She developed a special bond with my dad. He was scared to death of her until one day, my mom forced him to sit down and hold her. That's all it took! She could love him unconditionally while he sat for hours with her and made funny faces to hear her laugh. She could be having a horrible day, but the second he'd walk in the room and she'd hear his voice, her hands and legs would start flailing. She'd be looking around for him. However, if anyone happened to have on a white coat, Lindsey would get as still anything. Only her eyes would move then. Because a white coat meant doctor or nurse to her. We knew that there were things going on in her little mind.

During this time, we began doing more research for a diagnosis. The genetic testing performed in the beginning came back normal. The doctors thought that perhaps she had a disorder called Dubowitz syndrome. If this was the case, we would have a 1 in 4 chance of having another child with the syndrome. We actually sent the information to Dr. Dubowitz himself, and he confirmed that she did not have that abnormality. The week we received that news, I found out that I was pregnant with

Logan. (I had previously miscarried two surprise pregnancies.) I'd always wanted four children. Our family was growing!

Logan's pregnancy was uneventful until the final month. I became sick with vomiting and ended up being admitted to the hospital with contractions. I was so dehydrated, they couldn't even get an IV in me. This was a very scary time. I knew all the things that could go wrong with a baby born even a month early. When they were finally able to get the fluids administered, the contractions stopped. We were able to wait another two weeks before I delivered him by C-section. I was so nervous! I just needed to know that he was going to be okay. Thankfully, he was a big healthy boy. His was my easiest delivery! So Ryan was six and Lindsey was four when Logan joined our family. By this time Lindsey could go around six hours at night without needing medical attention. It's a good thing, too, since we had a newborn in the house!

We still did not take her many places since she had such a depressed immune system. She would get so sick, so easily! We were still going to church separately. In fact, a pediatric nutritionist that we worked with at the hospital told me once that she would see me at church alone and felt so sorry for me that my husband didn't share my faith. Then one day David showed up teaching her Sunday school class. She was so surprised when she realized that the two of us were married because she never saw us together. That was just our reality. There was often a disconnect within our social circles. People either knew me or they knew him, but some didn't realize for years that he and I "went together!"

When Lindsey was five she had a really bad flu incident. She was terribly sick that time. A doctor asked me during that hospital stay if we wanted to place a "DNR- do not resuscitate" order for her. I wasn't ready for that because her overall health had stabilized. Again, because this had just become the normal for us, I was alone when it came time to make that decision. It was a common occurrence in our lives that she would have to be taken to the ER. Medical decisions and what would be "crazy stressful medical events" to a parent with a healthy child were just our everyday lifestyle. Since David worked fulltime, it wasn't uncommon for the brunt of the decisions regarding her care to be mine.

On the evening of October 3, 1993, I noticed that she was not feeling well and commented to David, "I think I'll take her to the doctor tomorrow." I held her a long time that night wondering if I should take her to the ER or if we could wait until the morning? We gave her extra breathing treatments that night. The next morning as we were getting ready to go, I noticed that she was really struggling to breathe. It wasn't anything that I hadn't seen before with her. However, one very unusual thing she did that morning as I dressed her, was to stretch her arms all the way straight out. This was not something she had ever been able to do. Due to her limitations, the muscles in her limbs were very tight. She stretched once and then went completely relaxed. I thought, "Oh my goodness!"

I didn't actually realize at the time, but during the drive to the hospital, she quit breathing. Upon arriving at the ER, it was obvious that she was critical. They took the two of us right in and immediately start working on her.

I stepped out to call David at his office, and I couldn't get my fingers to dial the number. When I finally was able to reach him, I told him that she was in bad shape and that he needed to come right away. After I'd made that phone call, I tried to return to the room with Lindsey. They wouldn't let me back in.

The doctor came out, and I asked, "Not this time?"

"Not this time," he sadly replied, "no, she didn't make it."

By the time David, my parents and some friends arrived she'd already passed away. October 4, 1993. When they did let us go into the room to see her, it was very painful because the medical personnel left the body as it was while they had worked on her. We saw all of the trauma and the tubes they used to try and resuscitate her. The doctor returned to show us the x-ray of her chest. It was completely white, for her lungs were completely full. There was nothing that could have been done.

We spent a while with her saying goodbye. Her funeral was two days later on a beautiful sun shining day.

We requested an autopsy because we had never been given an actual diagnosis. We wanted for them to learn from her, and we wondered if we could get any answers. We knew that she was so much more than anyone ever anticipated. She was more that the "vegetative state child" that we were told to expect. She reacted to visual, auditory, and tactile stimulus. She was happy and sad. She recognized people.

After the autopsy, a kind doctor sat down with us and told us that it was amazing that she lived as long as she did. With all of her medical struggles, her life span was a testament to the quality of care that we gave her. Not only did her thyroid gland not form correctly, but her thalamus gland did not completely form. The thalamus provides our T-cells, which fight infection. That's why her infections would go "full-blown!" Her lungs were heavily scarred from the 15 pneumonias in her short life. The wall of her heart never thinned out enough to allow for a good hard pump. So, she never had good blood flow. What ultimately killed her was a Shigella bacterial infection. It is an illness which usually causes stomach pain and diarrhea in healthy children. Because her immune system was so compromised, it went to her lungs and killed her very quickly.

After the death of his little sister, Ryan had a friend come over to play. I was able to witness a very dear moment between the two of them. Ryan was able to express his grief. He wasn't crying. He was groaning while the other child held his head in her lap and rubbed his hair. A moment of pure sweetness, to see a pair of seven-year-olds consoling each other.

Throughout Lindsey's life, I dug my heart and my heels deeper into God. I learned to understand that His Holy Spirit interpreted my groaning. I often did not have the words to pray, but knew that He would give words to my needs and interpret my heart to God. I drew in and grew closer to Him.

We had a great network of friends and family who helped to carry us through. I did research on marriages with children who have severe disabilities and found that they fail 90-95% of the time. David and I made sure that we guarded our time together as a couple. We went out to lunch regularly. We tried to get away for an over-night trip for just the two of us once a year. We had a very open line of communication, and there was never any doubt that we were committed to holding our family together. There was no other option for us.

Logan was such a pistol of a toddler. David wanted to be finished having kids. I knew in MY heart that I wasn't done. We had another miscarriage and then I became pregnant with our daughter Paden who was born in 1997. At this time I was 34. Our whole community rejoiced at the birth of a healthy little girl.

Our family was complete. With the passing of one child, it would never be whole. We were changed by the life of Lindsey. We were refined and made stronger. God, her Creator, who fearfully and wonderfully knit her together in my womb, was undeniably glorified in her life.

David often explained when people asked about our difficulties, "We never ask God, 'Why us?' Instead we ask, 'Why not us?' Who ever said WE should be sheltered from suffering and trials." This was our reality, so the question remained, "What needs to be done to handle the problems of today?"

I knew when Lindsey was alive that God doesn't want babies to suffer. Sin came into the world and causes us pain and suffering. Satan is just wanting to get us. We are born into this world with many things already set in motion. Can God move mountains? Yes. Does He daily move them out of my life to make it easier? Maybe. I struggle with that notion that He removes hardship simply to make our paths smooth. He gives us the choice of how we will respond. God is all powerful. Yes. My question is, Will I remain faithful no matter what? Will I praise Him in the storm? If I don't get MY way, MY choice, My answer, MY decision, MY wants...am I going to remain faithful? How will I respond?

When God says, "No." Are we equally filled with praise when our prayers are not answered to our liking, as when God answers our requests per our desires? Would I still be rejoicing if God had said, "No?"

Bottom line, we are here on this Earth to glorify God. I don't understand that there is a way not to glorify Him. He wants us to honor Him anyway. No matter what. When you have trials where does your faith lie? God gives us opportunity to choose Him.

I thought we had come through the worst of the storm and nothing could compare to what we had survived. Little did I know that the future would once again test my faith and my strength.

David

On October 21, 2003, David had a colonoscopy. At the time we were thinking, "Okay, we are just going to see if anything is abnormal." After many years with Lindsey, we learned that you don't let your mind play games about symptoms and predictions. You have tests, wait for results, and then move forward. You refuse to go down the road of "what ifs." David had been anemic. Our doctor recommended we start with a colonoscopy to see where the anemia might be coming from. We knew that anemia can correspond with colon issues, so we decided to find out if there was anything more going on.

When the doctor came out after the procedure, I was alone. I'm always alone when these things happen. This is what the doctor told me, "We hit a complete blockage.

We could not even get the scope through. So, it will most likely be cancer. We will be taking him into surgery as soon as possible."

I was shaking. I realized, Immediate Surgery! They don't do that if it's not a big deal. We weren't even given the option of going home today and scheduling surgery later in the week. Here we were. It was happening, right now!

It was around 10:00 in the morning. My first thought was that the kids were at school, and I needed to make arrangements for them. Next, I started calling people to inform them that he was having surgery, and it was most likely cancer. I called my parents. Then I called the church office. I called David's brother and sister in Oklahoma, and they immediately began the 5 ½ hour drive to Lubbock.

I went back to sit with David and meet the surgeon. He and David started talking. They struck up this immediate friendship, sharing common interests and stories. Then Dan Rouse and Jeff Smith, both friends and ministers from our church arrived.

By 1:00 p.m., David's 2-3 hour surgery began. As I entered the waiting area, a crowd had already formed. Family and friends were so numerous that we spilled out into the lobby of Covenant Hospital. Doyle Gillam, who had become a surrogate father to David when his dad died when he was 21, was there with his wife, Louise. Sheri Wolfe, who'd recently had a colposcopy, was trying to be reassuring about the chances that they'd caught David's cancer early. We waited and we prayed.

When the surgeon walked out, he looked at me and said, "It's as bad as it gets." It was a very stunning moment, because no one was expecting, "It's as bad as it gets!" The cancer was all throughout the colon, in his abdomen, in the bottom of his lungs, and all over his liver. His abdomen was filled with cancer cells. He again said, "It's as bad as it gets...."

I was so surprised. We were 40 years old! We were all stunned, in complete shock. The very devastating news that my husband had six months to a year to live had been delivered.

A good friend brought me back to the here and now by telling me, "You need to get Ryan now. Word travels fast." So she was able to get hold of our 17-year-old son at school and get him to the hospital. I told him it was bad.

So much of the day was a blur. I have no recollection of how Logan and Paden got home from school. People just stepped in and did what they had to do to help a friend through times like these.

I wanted the doctor to tell David the news. There were just the three of us...David, Ryan and me in the hospital room then. Ryan was old enough to need to know everything. At 17, he needed to know.

The doctor repeated the statement, "It's as bad as it gets," to my husband and our oldest son. "You have probably six months to live, I don't expect you to be here a year from now."

David said, "Really? Well, Okay. Okay."

The doctor walked out, and I can only explain it as one of those surreal experiences, an out-of-body-moment where you don't think it's you standing in the room, but yet you know that you are. My mind was just reeling and racing!

"Whoa! He's telling me that my husband's is going to die soon. I've got three kids to raise." These and so many other thoughts were just racing through my mind. Racing thoughts! "How do I tell my kids? What am I going do? How do I do THIS?"

Because of the nature of our family and our particular church culture, there were a lot of people around while all of this was going on. Maybe that was a good thing. Maybe that helped to just kind of solidify what was happening. Someone told me later how quiet the halls of our church were that afternoon. There was a lot of sadness and a lot shock. We were all just grieving together. When our extended family started arriving, there was so much support for one another. There was so much love.

Then began the next journey of figuring out how to explain what was going on to a six-year-old Paden and an eleven-year-old Logan. How do you deliver this news to your young children? They were each at different developmental stages.

I told Logan that Dad had cancer and that he was very sick. "He will always have treatments, from now on," I told him. I didn't give him any kind of timeline or an end date. I explained to Paden that Daddy had an illness that he would never get well from. "He will never get well from this," is what I said to her.

I told each of them that if they ever had ANY questions about this they could ask me. I promised to tell them exactly what was going on. "I'll tell you what's happening and I'll explain it to you the very best I can," I said. I made sure to tell each of them that, alone with just the two of us.

Paden's first question, oddly enough, was, "Momma, what does righteousness mean?" Sweet girl! Who even knows where that came from?

At first, David was not really interested in taking cancer treatments. He had watched his mother suffer through them when she died of colon cancer. He didn't want to go through that, but his attitude was still positive. It reminded me a lot of our time with Lindsey. "Okay, what do we do now?" First things, first. He was so under nourished because of the blockage and the anemia. There were so many things to deal with all at once!

One interesting thing that exemplified David's spirit was that he continued to be such a driving force in each area of his life. He was a strong personality and understood that, "This is what we've been given to do...so we will do it." His goal had always been to go home and be with God. So, he would just do that very thing sooner than he had planned.

He was in the hospital about two weeks. His brother, sister, and I all took turns staying the night with him. They needed time with him, as well. We gave the kids a few days off from school but really tried to keep their schedules as normal as possible. The comment was made by the hospital staff, that when someone was looking for David's room, they could just follow the laughter. Just follow the laughter. People left his room feeling encouraged. That's just how he was. Follow the laughter!

There were lots of tears, as well. I kept returning to the thoughts, "Really? I'm 40 years old. I'm not supposed to have to do this. I don't want to do this. I do not want to go down this road. I don't want to make this journey. I want to keep living life and having fun!"

My prayers during this time were confusing and the words were hard. We had no doubt that the intercessory prayers of other people were carrying us through this time.

I quickly shifted into task-mode. I'd wake up and ask, "Okay, what needs to be done to get through today?" I was a stay-at-home mom, and David worked on commission. Our only bread winner now had a terminal diagnosis. How are we going to live for the next six months? The next year or two years? How are we going to do that?

David finally did decide to take cancer treatment. He changed his mind when a doctor encouraged him to give it a shot considering he was so young. I wanted him to, but I knew it had to be his decision. The chemotherapy treatments worked to give David relief from the symptoms and helped him to be more comfortable. After the surgery he had finally been able to eat because the blockage had been removed. He gained some weight and began feeling a little better. He tolerated the chemo treatments well.

We went in after three months and the doctor said, "David, your treatment is as good as it gets." That was good to hear! The doctors were especially watching the tumors on his liver, knowing that's what would eventually kill him. There were golf ball sized tumors all over. He went through the treatment, but at about six months its effectiveness started waning. However, a new drug was then added to his chemo regimen that really made a difference!

At this point, he started feeling better again and tried going back to work for a while. Before all this happened, things had been set in motion for David to take a new position in his company. We thought he would begin the transition of moving, rotating and spending two weeks in Albuquerque, NM and then back in Lubbock for two weeks. That obviously couldn't happen now. They had downsized his local office the week after his surgery. The company really did go above and beyond in many ways, but David just didn't have the desire to spend what time he had left working in an office doing long term financial planning for other people.

One day out of the blue, he asked me, "What's wrong with you? Are you angry? What's wrong are you mad?"

"Yeah, I'm mad."

"Well, are you mad that you are going to be a young widow?" He gave me all kinds of permission early on to get my anger out into the open.

"Yeah, I'm mad! I'm mad that you didn't go to the doctor sooner. I'm mad that, that life insurance test that you took *three* years ago that said your liver enzymes were high and you never followed up on it. I'm mad that you are leaving, and I've got to raise these kids alone. I'm mad about all of that!"

He just let my anger have a voice. He let me have a voice. He was really good to let me have my own emotions, apart from his.

I felt the priority of my role at this point was to support him in *what* he wanted to do and in *how* he wanted to live the time he had left. Along with this, I tried my best to be sure that the kids were okay.

David, true to his nature, began looking for ways to reach out to others and tell his story. He was determined to share what God was teaching him. Living in amazement of how cancer had afforded him this opportunity, he honored and glorified God in ways that he had never before experienced. He spoke publicly to many different people in various places and situations.

David often had people ask him, "Why haven't you prayed to be healed?"

He would tell them, "I have been healed. I am healed. My physical body may be dying, but I'm healed of my sin."

David's strength and zest for life even during his illness came from his deep faith in God. He would say to those who asked how he was handling it so well, "I've got just as many 'todays' as you've got." He had supported our family by helping others develop long term retirement planning. He would say, "We should all tend to those plans, but we are not promised anything more than right now. I've been told that my amount of days is going to be shorter than expected, but what's important is how we finish. How can we finish life well?" This resonated with members of his family who were really involved with the Special Olympics. Their catch phrase for that year was FINISH. David had the same goal.

We traveled around together for his speaking engagements. During these months, I quit going to the gym, quit doing many things that I was used to doing. When we heard "six months to live" my focus totally shifted to how WE were going to spend this six months to a year. We had tons of frequent flyer miles, so we took the kids on trips. We took Ryan to Washington, D.C. and spent almost a week with him. Logan and Paden wanted to go to the ocean. So we went to Playa del Carmen and played on the beach. We used up every frequent flyer mile we'd accumulated, all this between his speaking at tons of events and different churches. David always wanted me to go with him because often he didn't feel well. So, I went to everything. When the one year mark loomed closer, I was the one who started wimping out. I was tired! He was invigorated! While I didn't want to take that from him, we had moved from this being the 200 yard dash to the 10,000 meter race, the most grueling of all races! Life was a marathon, and (for my sake at least) we had to pace ourselves. I told him that I couldn't continue at that speed, it was too hard on me.

Ryan had since graduated from high school. With our encouragement for him to continue on with his dreams, he left for Harding University in Searcy, AR in August of 2004. It was hard to take him to college by myself when David was in the middle of a treatment. But, as always, we made it work and did what was needed.

We'd soon survived a whole year! When October 2004 rolled around we took David's surgeon out to eat for the one year anniversary of his diagnosis. David was still doing some speaking engagements, but spent the majority of his time at home with me. We had to learn how to make space for each other, all the while trying to make every day count. It was during these months that I earned my "Life and Health" insurance license, and we moved David's business into my name so I'd have a career opportunity after he was gone. Studying for that was like learning a new language. I got through all the studying, testing, and licensing only because it was something I needed to do for the future of my family.

We tried to live life as normal as possible, except for the glaring fact that Dad didn't go to work but went to treatments. The two of us arrived at a point where we allowed each other more space. The treatments lasted 4-5 hours, just sitting in a chair. One day he looked at me and said, "I'm okay here. You can go." Treatments then became his space. He'd call his family. He'd talk to different pastors that came. He also had a community of friends there. The kids still need me to be mom and taxi driver. Logan and Paden needed me to take care of them, too. I was still the one who made sure they were where they needed to be.

During this time, David did genetic testing. Because he was a 40-year-old, third generation, stage 4 colon cancer patient, obviously there had to be a genetic link. David had a maternal cousin die from the disease the month he received his diagnosis. Within that family there is history of pancreatic, uterine, ovarian and colon cancer. They tested a tumor for seven markers, all of which came back negative. However, we had no doubt that it was genetic. This made us worry about our kids. It's a daunting question... Is it a matter of "IF" or is it "WHO and WHEN?"

In July of 2005, we were going to New Mexico to take Logan to camp Blue Haven and decided that a trip to Yellowstone would be a great idea. The conversation on the way included Lance Armstrong's one-year diagnosis and the fact that he was still alive. David was wondering, "How long can this medicine keep me going? How much longer will I still feel decent?" We knew he'd never be up to full strength, but we carried on living. We enjoyed that trip together, though sometimes he'd stay at the camp site to rest. That was a big trip! We spent almost two weeks camping. That's enough to wear anyone out!

In August, I started noticing he was not feeling as well. Some things were changing. He began staying in bed more. I could tell that he was hurting a lot. He went in for a check-up, and we were able to tell the doctor about the changes. He prescribed a really strong pain reliever. That was the first time I remember David really crying. He said, "I don't think I'm ever going to feel good again." He worried about becoming addicted to the pain medicine. The doctor reassured him, that it would be fine since he was taking the medicine for the very reason it was intended. I remember sitting in our living room, in our little red chairs, with him worrying. He was right after all—he never did feel better.

My niece had started modeling, and I went on a trip with her around this time. David began the testing procedure for another experimental drug that week. I was gone for five days and returned to notice a marked difference in him. He had been given the news that he wasn't a candidate for that treatment because his numbers weren't good. Back was the grey coloring, the gaunt look of his face, and the swollen abdomen. He did not look good at all. They tried to go in and drain off fluid to give his lungs and abdominal organs some relief. He wasn't even a candidate for that. The fluid was in hundreds of pockets, which would take hundreds of needle sticks.

We were now well into the fall of 2005. We took a trip to the OU vs. UT game with some friends. If you knew David, you knew what a huge Oklahoma University fan he was, and this was always the football game of the year. Then, we went to visit Ryan at Harding. By this time, David was really not feeling well. He was able to do a few things and would then have to go in and nap. We visited his brother's church where David tried preaching one morning. We weren't sure if he would even make it through the lesson. He seemed confused, emotional, and had a hard time concentrating. Later, much to his amusement, we figured out that he had taken his night time meds, which included a strong sleep aid. It was amazing he could even stand!

People often asked, "What is the hardest part about all of this?" The hardest part for me was knowing I was losing the one I wanted to grow old with. I would say, "I am raising my kids to be strong, independent, and to move on. David was the one I wanted to spend my life with and he won't be here much longer." Accepting that he was dying was hard. Children growing up and leaving is a normal part of life. But he was my ONE to spend a life with.

I learned to tell those who asked how I was surviving that I am simply a vessel. I am nothing more than a vessel. I keep myself full of God and of what He offers. That is what carries me. The footsteps I leave are actually HIS and HE carries me the whole way.

That Tuesday morning, after that trip, we went in for a check-up. The doctor, with whom we had developed a strong relationship, came in and said, "Okay we are done. How do you want to do this?"

David asks, "What do you mean? 'Done...'"

"We were done with chemo. No more."

David said, "I'm not done. I'm not ready to be done. I still want to fight and keep moving forward."

The doctor's response was, "I thought you'd say that."

It was decided that his body could handle a half dose of chemo. That ended up wiping him out. It just completely wiped him out. He was not doing well at all. We went back the next week.

The doctor said, "Call hospice, not for you, but for your wife."

I called Ryan and then David's siblings to tell them that he was going down quickly. David had always been very close with his siblings. We had spent a lot of time with them and saw them for holidays. We all kept the roads that lead from our house to theirs well used. They all started coming knowing we were calling in Hospice. Our house became a revolving door. People wanted to come by. Friends. Family. Co-workers. So many people.

David became very spiritual. His conversations with people were broken in and out. They all came to see him and to tell him how much he meant to them. Our last week together was spent allowing others to be with him. I tried to have some more in depth conversations with him, but he had such a hard time focusing for any length of time. We found out later that was because of the toxins in his body.

By the time Ryan came, David was pretty much out of it. He was given a dose of Ritalin to help him be able to focus so they could have their time together. Logan became very tired of all the visitors, and would go to his friends' houses more often. My sister and her family came in that Saturday, and that was very comforting to everyone. They were so good for Paden. They hugged on her and ministered to each of us in their own way. David's brother and sister were here during this last week.

One of my favorite stories from that time happened one night as his brother was helping him into bed. David said, "The door is open!" When his brother asked him if he wanted him to close the bedroom door, David pointed to the ceiling and said, "No. The door is open. So, I need a circle of protection for my family." His brother reassured him, "It is okay. We are here. You've got it. We are all here for them."

Cline and Gerald Paden (amazing Bible scholars from our church) and their wives all came over one evening. David asked Gerald, "You know, I've been wondering...what language do you think we will speak in heaven?" Gerald looked at me with a tear in his eye and said that he'd never been asked that before. He guessed that maybe we'd speak the language of angels. That satisfied David.

Saturday morning David got up to take a bath and commented, "I have good roommates here. One of them is wearing socks." I thought then that the only person who ALWAYS wore socks was our Lindsay. When she was in the hospital, I'd keep two socks on her.

I asked him, "What are you seeing?" There was this feeling of him coming in and out of this world. All the while there was a constant stream of people coming and going. We really tried to honor that because having people around him was David's nature.

I sat with him a lot through this time. He'd lean over and say, "The angels are here. I hear the music." At one point I left the room for a minute and was told that he was asking for me. When I got up close to his face, he looked away and said, "You're not who I'm looking for." All that night, he greeted people only he could see. He blew kisses...said things like, "hey, looking good..." "Hi,

Momma!" and kissed and greeted. By the next morning, that had stopped.

It was Sunday morning. I told him, "It is okay now. Go peacefully." He'd always said that he wanted to get hit by a bus the day before he was scheduled to die of cancer. He wanted it to be quick like that, and it was just almost that fast. He was out speaking publicly two weeks to the day before he died. On October 30, 2005 my husband David passed on very peacefully, surrounded by his family and friends.

The funeral was a celebration. David had teased that he wanted his funeral to be seminar style with 8X10 glossy pictures of him passed around with hot dogs and popcorn served in the church lobby. We brought it down a bit and only had 5X7 glossies of his face with his autograph for the funeral brochure. The first song played was "Boomer Sooner." A friend popped open a Dr. Pepper in his honor, and many shared just what David had meant to them.

Then it all got quiet. The visitors were gone. The kids were back at school. The house was silent....that was the hardest part. Life gets back to normal for the rest of the world. I was trying to work from home a bit, but that was very disjointed. It was not much more than just opening mail and doing the bare minimum. We did some grief counseling as a group. I forced my kids to go, like it or not. Logan went, but didn't want to be there. Paden was happy to go. That counseling taught us what we were feeling was normal in grief. I just remember repeatedly telling myself, "If I don't do this well, my kids will suffer worse. It doesn't just affect me, but my whole family. I have to do this well...I have to do this well...I have to get up and put one foot in front of the other and walk through a day." One of the scriptures that I used to lean heavily upon is from Psalms - God is my fortress and refuge. I can be protected when I go into HIS refuge. HE protects me. He puts His angels' wings around me. He surrounds me with His love and His fortress. He is my safe place. Yet, that belief and comfort did not mean that I was magically relieved of all the pain.

It was Ryan that summer who brought to my attention that I was spending too much time alone in my room. Even when the kids were home I was withdrawing. I found out that as a part of my grief, noise became very much of an irritant to me. I caught myself being very depressed and unmotivated. I did not want to get up and put one foot in front of the other, but I did. I knew that that first year was not the time to make big changes. The hardest part of that year was being alone. It is an aloneness. It's not loneliness. It's BEING ALONE. However, He is faithful, and God protected me! I remember saying, "You know, Satan...you are NOT getting me. I'm God's child. You are not getting me. You throw a lot at me, but you are NOT getting me. So, go elsewhere. Just go somewhere else. 'Cause playing in this court ain't gonna get you anywhere."

I did a study of the book of Daniel after David died. It taught me so much about the concept of "being refined". God refines me. I, like gold, am put into the fire in order to be refined, purified, and made stronger. The fires, tests, and trials that I have been through continue to refine me. I just want to continue being refined more and more. David showed me how to go through the fire of life and NOT let the fires char and disfigure me. I am always growing, always learning, and always changing.

From a mom's eyes, the hardest part of my refining (and theirs) was watching my children and wondering if they would be okay. How would they deal with this loss of their father? Ryan was attending Harding University at this time, and I wondered, "How's he doing in school? Is he allowing himself to grieve? Is he sharing it with somebody?" I learned that my children didn't have to share their grief with me just as long as they were sharing, coping, and dealing with it somehow. I found out later that Ryan was writing poetry and sending it to a friend. He'd worked on some photographs and sent me some pictures of us while David was still alive. He was finding his own way of coping with his dad's death.

Logan and Paden both stayed out a week from school here in Lubbock. He died on a Sunday, the funeral was that Wednesday, and they returned to school the following Monday. So, it was time once all the family left, for them to get back to their normal routine. Logan, in particular had friends who thought he should be acting differently, showing more grief or sadness. They didn't understand that school was THE place where he could just be himself. It wasn't like home, where he didn't have to, as he explained to me, "take a deep breath before walking through the door." School was the place where Dad wasn't involved...where he could just be normal. Logan got a lot of flak for that. People are just insensitive sometimes. For example, all but one of his teachers said not to worry about his grades. When I did go into the school office to give them some paper work for Logan's absences, I was told that "Oh they don't get a week for that (the death of a parent). They only get three days." I had to take a few deep breaths and quickly conclude my business with that particular person!

Now, David has been gone for eight years, and my kids talk to me about his death more than ever before. But, it is an ongoing process for the three of them. I learned, when Lindsey died, that children grieve initially, but have to continue to grieve as they mature. That really stinks! What a 13-year-old comprehends is so different than what an 18-year-old is able to process. As they mature, they will go through a different grief progression. Paden was only eight, and there are a lot of "our" memories that she doesn't have; therefore, her grief has been a bit simpler. Ryan still goes through it. I'll watch him still have pieces of it that he will go through. Logan, just this year, talked about it.

He told me, "Dad asked me to go fishing with him in August that last time he ever went out on a boat and I said, 'No.' Just 'cause I wanted to go play with my friend. I didn't say 'Yes' to my Dad. I guess that I just got used to him being sick." That was really where we were. We'd determined at that point that cancer was not going to direct our lives. We couldn't let it change everything we did. It became the new normal. Logan admitted, "I'd almost forgotten that Dad was sick."

Ryan wishes now that he would have come home the summer in between his freshman and sophomore years, but he didn't. I tried to remind them that we were all making the best decisions that we knew how, at the time. We just can't have those "shoulda...woulda...couldas..." They will eat you up and spit you out with regrets. You can't live that way.

I continue to pray a lot that God gives me the words that He wants me to say. I pray for His words AND His timing. This is a very common prayer for me, "Please give me the words and the timing, to know what to say and when to speak it."

As a single mom, during that time, I can say with certainty that it is a hard thing to make ALL the decisions for the family. All the decisions were mine, period! That was hard! Simple things like having a major hail storm and trying to figure out how to fix the roof and get the car repaired. The heater went out a month after David died, then the dryer. I talked to a woman who told me to develop a "staff." So I did just that. I had a list of friends and church family that I could call when I was in need of a particular kind of help. I called on my staff often. Then I realized, that as a single Christian woman, I never wanted there to even be a hint of anything inappropriate going on. Most of those on my staff of helpers were the husbands of friends and sisters in Christ. I had to be purposely respectful of that.

Being single was very challenging. In marriage, you have the other person to pick up the slack when you are weak. One is stronger in a certain area, and two are able to balance each other. I suddenly didn't have that. More than anything, perhaps we missed David because he always brought the "FUN" into our lives. We just missed the fun! So, we put one foot in front of the other and life just kept on going down the road.

We don't understand the ways of God. I have never invited chaos, but it is in my world. It comes at me. Why? Teen pregnancy, divorce, suicide, mental disorders, have all happened within my immediate family. Where does loss of jobs, no income, living off government assistance all fit into the plan of God for my life? We know the story of Job and that he was faithful man. We know that Satan was allowed to tempt and hurt him, but God would not allow Satan to HAVE Job. I have always known that I was under God's protection. No matter what horrific events were swirling around me, I am God's child above anything else. Ultimately, God has me in the shelter of His wings. My pivotal point in my walk with God was after David got sick. My question changed from "Do I trust Him to take care of my needs?" to "Do I <u>know</u> that He is taking care of my needs and will provide?" We were okay.

Mitzi

In October 2007, two years after David died, I had the opportunity to go to work. It was a perfect fit for my situation. The people who offered me the job had been family friends for years. In fact, they were the ones who drove my car home after Lindsey died.

One day while David was in the hospital, he mentioned to these friends, "Hey, don't forget Jana. She might need a job someday." So they gave me an open invitation.

Working was such a huge adjustment for me. In the beginning, they let me just work school hours. I had tons of flexibility, and it seemed to be a perfect fit. However, the challenging part was figuring out when in the world I was going to do all the things I normally did while Logan and Paden were at school. When could I go to the grocery store, run errands, all the other ordinary chores that filled my days? The timing and the pace of it were so very difficult for me. When I asked a friend who had lived on a foreign mission field, she assured me that when she, as a mom, went back to working full-time, it was more difficult than moving to a foreign country. That's what I was feeling, culture shock! It was reassuring to know that I wasn't the only one who found juggling kids and a fulltime job exhausting. I really think it depends on the person. Some women seem to fall right into it and thrive. For some of us though, it goes against our nature. It was a really hard transition for me to be 45 years old and never having worked fulltime outside of my home. I called myself a dinosaur! Old and out of date.

Around this same time Logan started really struggling. He was acting out and began running away. To top things off, my parents divorced right after their 50th wedding anniversary. I was simply trying to manage life from one hard, gut-wrenching event to the next. Just trying to smile some along the way.

Through all of this, a woman named Mitzi Brown was one of my very close friends. She had walked through so many of these trials with me. Come to find out, she'd not been feeling well for months. She had various symptoms, but because of an unfortunate health insurance situation, she hadn't had any testing done. I noticed one day when I touched her arm that she felt so thin and that her coloring just wasn't right. I knew then, unfortunately from experience, that they should be concerned. I was trying not to jump to conclusions just because of what we'd experienced in our family. But, I knew enough to be worried!

A couple weeks later, after having been out of town for Christmas of 2008, I was told that Mitzi was in the hospital. As I entered her room, the first thought that struck me was that she looked just like David had looked a mere two weeks before he died. I had to stop and catch my breath before I could take another step. The family told me that the doctor was on his way to talk to them and asked me to stay. Mitzi was sitting up talking with her husband Bob. The two of them were describing the tests that had been run, and as the doctor came in they asked me again, "Jana, please stay."

The doctor started explaining what he was able to understand at that point concerning her situation. As one who had lived through similar circumstances, I watched and listened, and as he talked, I could see by the looks on Bob and Mitzi's faces that they were having a really hard time wrapping their minds around what exactly the doctor was saying. I was able to ask the doctor if he could explain things in maybe a little different way. I'm the type that will ask for information repeatedly until it makes sense to me. I can remember him telling them the gravity and serious nature of the situation. I knew by the way she looked that it was not good.

I remember when I left that day, Mitzi said, "Jana, I'm scared! I'm so scared!"

I told her, "I know." I mean what else do you say?

I remember hearing her ask the doctor, "Am I going to get to raise my babies?"

I talked to her one other time, very briefly. Thinking that she had lymphoma, they moved her into an isolation ward in preparation for cancer treatments. We were only able to wave to one another, and she told me jokingly, "We're gonna have to go wig shopping pretty soon."

Within a day or two after that, she coded and was placed on life support. I did my best at that point to really try to and be there for her family. There are so many things that are involved in hospitalization, forms, insurance etc. It gets so overwhelming to deal with the technicalities all the while your loved one is in a hospital bed, fighting for life.

While on full life-support (respirator, ventilator and kidney dialysis), they were able to temporarily bring her to consciousness so Bob and their children Taylor (16) and Michaela (13) could talk with her a bit. She was so sick that no one, neither nurse nor doctors, wanted to risk moving her to do any kind of further testing or scans in order to find out what was *actually* wrong with her. They were afraid that she would not survive the simple task of moving her from that bed.

One day while I was there I noticed a very particular smell in Mitzi's room. I'd never noticed it before. It had kind of a sweetness to it. I was told later that it was the smell of death. Apparently, sometimes as the body is dying it emits a sweet aroma. When I asked the ICU nurse about it, she said that yes, they smell it all the time.

Her family really struggled with the decision to take her off of life-support. There was evidence of brain function. However, Mitzi's body, much like David's, didn't have the strength to support it.

They eventually decided to risk moving her to get an MRI full body scan. After that move, she went downhill very quickly. I was there with Mitzi's parents, her husband, Bob, and a couple of other good friends when the doctor came in to give the results of the MRI. He started from head to toe, pointing out all the places they thought were cancerous—the brain, the heart, the liver, the kidneys.

When he arrived at the bone in her leg, and described it as looking like a star burst, I finally spoke up and asked, "So where is it NOT in her body?"

The doctor replied, "Nowhere." Then he flipped the monitor off and said, "That's enough! She will not survive this."

On the evening of January 21, 2009, they made the decision to take her off life-support. Just her family was in the room as she passed away. The hall way was filled with people lined-up wanting desperately to support them and love on them as they came out of her room.

Now here I was with another young person that I loved, my dear friend, with her life here on Earth at an end. I got through this additional cruel blow to my heart by remembering that this life is so temporal. We each have a choice when tragedy strikes. Do we stick with God or leave Him? I, personally, can't imagine walking these paths without Him. My question is, "How do you survive without Him carrying you through tragedy?" I can't imagine.

Bob

During the late Fall of 2009, (the same year Mitzi died) the leadership of the church where my family and Bob & Mitzi's family had attended for years was looking to start a ministry for older singles within the church. Most of the time, it seems that singles ministries are geared toward those a bit older than college age, but just hadn't yet found Mr. or Miss Right. What about those of us that are in mid-life and find ourselves single? Where do we fit? I often found myself frustrated with the absence of the "widow" box. You know, when you are filling out an identification form of some kind, and it asks you to check a box that best described your status: Single, Married, Divorced? Where was the allusive Widow Box? It's like we didn't exist or something! Anyway, some letters were sent out asking a few of us if we'd consider helping with this kind of ministry. Ugh! I was indeed single, but had not even considered moving on to dating. It was not even on my radar. I was too busy raising kids. I wasn't going to bring just anybody home to my kids. I was working. I was busy attending their sports and activities. Who had time for being single? Who had time for dating? Not me!

Bob (Mitzi's husband who had also been asked to lead the group) and I compared notes about the possibilities of whether or not God was leading us to work with others in similar circumstances. First of all, the letter called us old and then called us single! Bleh! Bob says that he threw his letter directly in the trash but ended up coming to the first meeting anyhow. Honestly, neither of us were really interested in a singles group because we still had our friends, the same ones we'd had for the past 20 years. We already had our support group. I'd always said that if God wanted me to have another husband, he'd have to drop him in my lap.

I do remember Bob telling me when Mitzi died, "I'm gonna need your help in the next few months." I thought cautiously to myself, "Yes you will, but I have to make sure I do this right." I sure didn't want anyone thinking that my motives for helping Bob and his family were anything less than pure. These were my friends, my family's friends, my Christian friends. I didn't want it to ever be perceived as something more than helping a friend.

So, as I was living my life, working, taking care of my kids, attending church activities, I realized that I began missing that deep, intimate relationship of a marriage. I had a great community around me. However, I really missed having that one person to share my life. Because that's really what a marriage is...you share life. The absence of that person, for me, was the aloneness that I felt since David's death. I was missing that sharing of deepest emotions with someone.

The other thing I considered at this time was, "God, am I serving You in Your body as a single woman, as *well* as I could be serving You if I were married?" I was used to being part of a pair. David and I were married 20 years. That was most of my adult life. I was really struggling with the feeling of not being able to serve *well* as a single woman, because just living life was taking so much of my energy. Just doing life! That struggle was going on in my heart and head at the same time as this new older singles group was trying to get started. We did begin meeting together, and life went on down the road.

A few curious things happened around this time. I remember I saw Bob talking to another woman at one of those meetings, (just talking, mind you), and I got a jealous pang. "What was that?" my thoughts raced, "Why did I even notice that?" Next, I went to visit David's sister, and she asked me straight out, "So, are you thinking about dating?" She had never asked me anything like this before. I just stood there feeling shocked and not knowing how to respond.

Before, my answer would always have been, "Nah, of course not." Now with my feelings toward Bob seeming to be in transition, I wasn't sure exactly what to say, or even think for that matter. (I found out later that right around Christmas Mitzi's brother told Bob that he thought it was time that Bob start dating.) God was at work even through the siblings of our spouses to begin bringing us together.

A group of us from church went out for dinner one night. As we finished up and began talking afterward, I was able to tell Bob that my sister's mother-in-law was dying exactly the same way that Mitzi died. She had all the same symptoms. They had recently received the autopsy report on Mitzi's illness. It was a very rare type of fungus that invaded her body and because she had a severely compromised her immune system (she probably had lymphoma), her body could not fight it off.

Gradually, through many shared conversations about raising families, working with the older singles group, Bob's daughter Michaela and my Paden becoming closer friends, and just living life. I began to notice that my heart beat with a little bit different rhythm when Bob came around. I began to feel the flutter of anticipation (I hadn't felt that in a really long time) when we would end up sitting near each other during worship. My friend Bob was quickly becoming so much more.

The next thing we know, the autumn of 2009 turned into the Christmas season. My extended family was kept away from visiting because of an ice storm. I'd promised Bob's son Taylor that I would come and see him play in a basketball tournament. Our daughters spent a lot of time together that holiday season. That naturally led to Bob's and my paths crossing much more frequently. My heart now *always* noticed when he was around. It would begin that erratic skip a beat rhythm as soon as he walked into the room. It wasn't long before my mind began agreeing with my heart.

How do two people who have shared so many trials and have gone up against the struggles of this life separately, begin to join their paths, join their families, and join their hearts? In looking back, it may have appeared to others that this all happened very quickly, but the two of us spent hours upon hours talking together. These were hours spent just sharing life.

One evening while the girls were hanging out together, Bob and I started talking about the singles ministry and he said, "You know I've been thinking. Well, I've sorta been wondering if, you know, I could be way off base here, but just thinking...that maybe there's more than a friendship between us." It took him a good little while to get it out, but I quickly reassured him that he was not off base. I was ready for a beautiful, crazy romance. He had indeed been dropped into my lap.

We knew that because we were both widowed, parents of teenagers, and ran in the same social circles that news or even rumors-of-news would travel fast. We needed to figure out quickly exactly where we stood right now in this relationship and where we were planning on going in this relationship.

So our first official date came on December 30th. We headed to a local, downtown restaurant. Oddly enough, December 30th was David's and my anniversary. When I mentioned this to Bob, he was so respectfully sensitive to that, he was ready to turn around and take me back home. I'd been a widow for four years, and it was okay to begin again. I feel like we talked miles that night. I know we talked for hours. We really were able to get everything out on the table and be completely honest about how we were each feeling. This good man, who I'd known for 25 years, was in love with me and I loved him back. We'd each buried a mate. We'd helped each other survive. That night we even took new steps through the grieving process. We cried together. We celebrated love together. We began a new chapter no longer alone, but together. By the time school started again in January, everyone knew that we were dating.

Early on the morning of Jan 21, 2009 I called Bob. He assumed that I was calling to tell him that I was thinking about him since it had been a year to the day since Mitzi died. That wasn't actually the reason for my call. I'd just learned that my Dad passed away suddenly in the middle of the night. I received the news at 3:30 that morning, so I'd already been over there with my Mom for a few hours.

During the week of Dad's funeral, my family was able to meet or in some cases, get reacquainted with Bob. My brother and Bob actually knew each other from their college years. My sister kept saying over and over, "Look how sweet he is to her!" This was just one more example of the nature of life. It moves forward! Just like having our first date on my wedding anniversary, my father dying on the anniversary of Mitzi's death showed that in no uncertain terms that life moves forward. It keeps on going. We either join it or get left behind.

I experienced one of my strongest grief moments soon after that. I was sitting around thinking one day, and having come to the decision that I was indeed going to move forward with Bob, it became clear that I had to put David in a different place. Having to close David's chapter in my life more completely was one of my most intense sorrows. He never goes away, we all understand that. He will always be part of my life and who I am because I grew up with him. I couldn't hold on to "what was" as strongly as I had been. I, like life, had to move forward to "what is." While I was single, I could hold on to what used to be and what I was missing and what wasn't there. I could live, be productive, and even enjoy life while holding on to the past. However, when I decide to move forward with another man, that new beginning was also and ending to what had been.

Thankfully, neither one of us had any apprehension about getting married. We knew it would be hard to join our families, but we knew we could do it. I knew that I could only marry a strong Christian person. That was of most importance.

Oddly enough we got engaged right before I had a previously scheduled hysterectomy in February. After four cesarean deliveries, I'd developed a lot of scar tissue and had chronic pain from that. Thinking ahead to my post-surgery recovery time, I decided to buy an extra TV so the kids could move their gaming system into the back room. That would provide some peace and quiet towards the front of the house where I would be resting. So, Bob and I made a trip to Sam's Club to get a TV. While we were there I just happened to mention, "Hey, they have jewelry here. Why don't we go take a look? Well, I like that ring. Wow, it's just my size. That works! There is a band that even had five stones for our five kids, just like we had talked about. Look at this one for you, Bob. Yep, it fits! Wrap 'em up!" And just as easy as that we had our wedding rings and new TV. We even had toilet paper, too. That filled our February. On March 13, 2010, with many friends and family cheering us on, we were married.

One of the most amazing things about my wedding day with Bob was found in the supportive presence of almost every member of David's family. I was so closely connected to each of them. We'd spent years of holidays and vacations together. To not only have their blessing but also to have their presence was truly amazing.

We didn't have a typical wedding ceremony. We did most all of the talking ourselves, so we didn't even have a preacher. We tried to really make it special for each of our children by including them in the wedding and giving them jewelry. It was a very open and honest time to share our love and joy with those around us. Afterwards, one friend commented that she felt like she'd been to a movie, "I laughed...I cried!" More than one man in attendance told me that ours was the best wedding they'd ever been to.

We spent our honeymoon in San Diego simply relaxing. There had been so many decision to make from which house we were going to live in, how to handle the finances, and how live with four teenagers under one roof. We needed a little peaceful time together to regroup.

People often ask about our kids and how they handled all of these changes. I can tell you this, being a step-mom is the hardest thing I have ever done. You've read my story. I have been through some pretty hard stuff. This was one of the hardest. In all fairness, my three children had four years since the loss of their dad. Mitzi had only been gone a little over one year. Women and men typically mourn differently. Men are generally ready to move on sooner than women. Bringing our kids along with that was hard on them. As we moved forward with that, I still find myself trying to determine my role as we continued striving to have a home of respect and love.

I know without a doubt that God provides a way of survival through every struggle. He provides help for me most often through amazing people that He places in my life. No matter what He gives me to handle (seemingly good or bad), He will always provide just the kind of help that I need to see me through.

What have I learned through all of this? I have learned that God continues to bless you, no matter what. I have learned that if you remain open to whatever is put in front of you, who knows what will come your way. Sometimes we want to have our own road map and direct our own course. All I know is that the only road map that I'm sure of is that I'm going to heaven. My route appears to weave and turn all over the place, but I know that my course is set straight towards Him. I'm not in the driver's seat. I don't determine the pace and I don't get to choose the state of the road. I am simply to be faithful as I travel. I want to honor and glorify God in whatever I do. I have also learned that no matter what happens, life keeps moving forward. Life just keeps on moving down the road. Some of my loved ones reached their final goal of heaven much sooner than I would have liked. My heart and my plans have been broken and changed. Through each twist and turn, my Father God has remained faithful. He gives and He takes away. Blessed be His name.

About the Author

Jana Shelburne-Brown is a producer/agent for Ashmore & Associates Insurance Agency. She is married to Bob – they have 5 children – Ryan 28 is married to Michelle, Logan 22, Taylor 22, Michaela 19, and Paden 17. Jana serves on the Leadership Training for Christ board and is active at the Sunset church in Lubbock, TX.

Five Seconds of Courage

a synopsis

Ann White

He reached down from on high and took hold of me; He drew me out of deep waters. Psalm 18:16

8:32 p.m. May 29, 2012 The Leonardo Hotel, Tiberias, Israel

I am a Christian, a Bible Study Leader, a Wife, a Mom, and a Grandmother.

And I. Am. Drowning.

These are the only words I can think of to adequately convey the despair in my soul that night. I was on what should have been a dream vacation with my son, Blake, visiting Israel and experiencing Scripture come to life through the teaching of my Pastor, Johnny Hunt. But all I could think of that night was, "my marriage is over." I was lost in a sea of confusion and grief, and without supernatural intervention, I was going under, fast.

It had been a long day of touring through an ancient seaport and Roman theatre in Caesarea, Mount Carmel, Megiddo, and the Valley of Armageddon. I had hoped that this trip would be a nice reprieve from the escalating tension between Mike and me, and had even gone so far as to leave my phone turned off in order to limit our communication. Blake, however, kept his phone on. Now, looking back, his desire to stay connected at home may have been one of the great catalysts God used to force my hand towards honesty, and ultimately towards healing. Despite hoping that the time away would be a good thing for our relationship, Mike and I, on our son's phone, managed to get into yet another fight. Hurtful words were spoken, we were a mess, and maybe the most tragic part was that nobody knew.

The most troubling result of hiding our struggles is that we become alone in them. Loneliness compounded with hurt is almost always a recipe for despair. My carefully crafted walls of protection had left me feeling completely alone, and I knew that if I didn't ask for help now, I never would, and Mike and I would be over. I had no idea how to move forward, I only knew that I could no longer stay where I was. As I prayed, God gave me exactly what I needed in that moment – five seconds of courage...

This was literally all I had, and with shaking hands I scribbled my fears and realities onto a sheet of hotel letterhead. I knew it was now or never, so as soon as I finished, I called Johnny and Janet to see if they were in their room. Janet answered, she was there, and I opened my door and headed out. I remember the emptiness of the hotel hallways as I walked. How could this be happening to me? How in the world did my beautiful family get here? Questions and doubts raced through my mind with each step, but I was resolute. I was terrified, but I was resolute.

I knocked on the door half hoping she wouldn't answer. But she did, and I all but shoved the note into her hands. The words quickly tumbled out, as she stood there bewildered, "I am desperate and have to tell someone the truth." She of course invited me in, but I wasn't ready for the face to face, I wasn't ready for a conversation. I was barely ready for what had just happened.

But it had happened, I had pushed through my fear long enough to invite someone into my deepest struggle. For you, this might not seem like much, but for me, it was everything. This was the moment I began my journey towards freedom.

You might be wondering, how I got to such a fractured place. I assure you, my steps were taken on an all too common path, well-worn with the footsteps of thousands before me. My personal journey is marked with the road signs of my false beliefs. Unfortunately, these signs did not direct me towards the life I wanted; they nearly led me to destruction. But thanks be to God, He has torn down these lies and replaced them with truth. It is likely that your story is nothing like mine, but you do have a story, and if like me, you have to come to believe some lies along the way, let's walk together. My prayer is that God will use my courage to help you find yours.

TRUTH: Sanctify them in truth, Your Word is truth.
John 17:17

I, like almost everyone, believed that my childhood and family were completely normal. In fact, studies show, that most children believe that their home life situation is the same as everyone else. Children of addicts believe that every parent is an addict; children of abuse believe that every home is abusive; you get the point. Our young minds shape our belief systems about family, love, marriage, God, and life as we experience it. These beliefs shape our choices. Now, before you judge this story as "another tale of someone blaming their parents for their mistakes," this is not that, not even a little. But if you are to understand how I came to such an isolated and broken place that I was ready to walk away from my marriage, you MUST understand that it was a journey of many subtle steps of wrong beliefs that led me far away from the life I wanted.

Both of my parents were married to someone else when they first met one another through work. My mother had two small boys and my father had a young son and daughter. They met, divorced their spouses, and married. Within two years, they had me. His, hers, and ours; we were the modern family. Mom told me later in life that the first five years of their marriage were great. Dad was good to my brothers, and he was fun to be around, happy, and faithful to her. After that, something changed within him. I can make guesses but the truth is I don't really know. The father that I knew was successful and a good provider, but he was also angry, self-absorbed, emotionally abusive through withholding love, verbally abusive, at times physically abusive, and unfaithful. My mother worked very hard to keep him calm and to accommodate his extreme behaviors. This shaped my lie of belief that a good wife accepts and accommodates the negative behaviors of her husband.

The strange twist to the story is that while he expressed these behaviors towards my mother and his two stepsons, he most often treated me like his little princess. I did not understand his favoritism, and his affection towards me seemed to come at the expense of others. This grew the lie of belief that if I am treated special, it will always come at the expense of others.

I looked up to my big brothers. Their mistreatment by my father was, and is, one of the greatest heartaches of my life. I would have given anything for my father to change, to the extent that I began to believe that his loving me was tied into his abuse of them. As a result of this, I developed a deep guilt complex, especially when it involved me receiving special attention.

Growing up, my family had on and off attended church. It was something we did because it was something everyone did. My earliest memories of going to the small Methodist church were that of resting my head in my mom's lap and drawing on the weekly bulletin. I had a Bible in my room that lived a patterned existence. It went to church with me once per week, and after that it rested upon a small table. It might as well have been a coaster or had blank pages. I was never taught or encouraged to read Scripture, and I was certainly never shown how to study it for understanding and application.

My people are destroyed from lack of knowledge.
Hosea 4:6a

Like many, I believed in God and in Jesus, or at least I believed in the parts that I knew about them. Being a Christian was a label I wore just as easily as I was an American. There was no relationship with God and certainly no responsibility on me. I believed He didn't really care that much about me and was too busy with more important matters. This reinforced the lies of belief that God did not care about me personally and that simply believing in God and Jesus was the same as being a Christian.

Over the years I have heard many mothers asking for prayer for their children to have Godly friends and influences. In fact, I have been one of those mothers. Looking back throughout my childhood, I cannot remember a single voice of spiritual influence in my world, not one. My fledgling faith was propped up by my shallow beliefs. God, in my mind, was distant yet loving, but He certainly was not involved with my life. Religion touched on the exterior only and as far as I was concerned, so did God.

I met Mike on the first day of school at Milton High. My family had only recently moved to Georgia, and I, not knowing the social rules of my new school, dressed up for my the first day wearing a skirt, blouse, and heels, in the land of blue jeans. Needless to say, I stood out. After a brief interaction with several members of the football team in the hallway, Mike smiled at me and offered to walk me to my class. A few months later, we both participated in a Christmas play performed at a local nursing home, and that was it. I was 14 years old and I was in love.

Mike was charismatic, warm, cute, upbeat, fun, and he was a senior. My lowly freshman status didn't seem to matter to him, and I found myself comfortably lost in his aura of confidence. More than anything else, Mike cared for me. He regularly found ways to demonstrate his care, and I, to this very day, have never known a more generous and caring man.

During my adolescence, my growing resentment of my father's "Princess" treatment gave me the courage to rebel against him. My extreme behavior and his hot temper began to clash, and the anger and abuse that had previously been focused on my mom and stepbrothers had now turned towards me. We would go from polar extremes of me receiving his full attention and love to him chasing me across the front yard in an attempt to hit me. My young mind began believing that the unhealthy extremes of his love were normal and that my mistreatment was just all part of the package. This fostered the lie of belief that I deserved to be mistreated.

Mike became my savior in nearly every sense of the word. He helped me escape my family's brokenness, he protected me from my dad, he made me look good, and he made me feel accepted. This grew within me the lie of belief that Mike, or any human, was going to meet all my needs.

We were young, and neither of us had healthy relationship examples. Translation: sex became a part of our equation. I was no longer an innocent, but despite our physical closeness, there was something between us that was lacking. Mike was everything I had ever wanted, and I so desperately wanted to be in love and to be loved. But since I had no idea what love really looked like, I settled for the lie that being wanted is the same thing as being loved.

Mike's charisma and strong work ethic opened the door for him to begin working in the insurance industry at a young age. Naturally, I joined him, and at age nineteen began selling insurance door to door. It was 1983 and it was completely acceptable to go up to someone's door and engage them in conversation about insurance, about anything really. People were much more open to interaction. Thankfully, I was too...

One particular day I was partnered with Miles Duley, and in between homes he asked me, "Ann, if you died today, do you know that you would go to Heaven?" Despite my having beliefs about God and had attended church, I had no idea if I would be admitted into Heaven. I answered him honestly and Miles then explained to me that according to the Bible, I could know for sure.

We talked for a few more minutes about what it meant to be "saved," and he shared with me that Jesus wanted to have every part of me. I liked the notion of being loved and accepted, and I knew that the life I was leading was not one that any "good, church-going Christian" would have thought acceptable, much less God.

After a bit more conversation Miles pulled the car over to the side of the road and led me in a simple prayer.

Praying out loud felt a little foolish, but it also felt like the most natural thing I had ever done. I admitted to God that I was a sinner, which wasn't hard for me to do. I confessed that I had tried to do my best but had fallen short, asked for His forgiveness for my sin, acknowledged my faith in Jesus to save me, and asked Him to come into my life to be my Lord and Savior.

If you declare with your mouth, "Jesus is Lord," and believe in your heart that God raised him from the dead, you will be saved. Romans 10:9

I did not hear angels singing (although I now have come to know that they were), and honestly, I didn't really have a drastic outward life change. But what did happen was that I began having an awareness of God's presence in me. It was terrifying and liberating at the same time. I also noticed that I began wanting very different things than I had before. I had always believed that being a Christian was a matter of simple belief, but the truth of salvation had exposed that lie. Now, however, without anyone to disciple me into this new life, my journey as a Christian became painstakingly slow. It wasn't until many years later that my transformed heart began to reflect a transformed life.

Do not conform to the pattern of this world, but be transformed by the renewing of your mind. Then you will be able to test and approve what God's will is—His good, pleasing and perfect will. Romans 12:2

Mike and I continued dating, but we had an on again, off again pattern. We both seemed to never be able to get over each other, and for this I am grateful. I continued selling insurance until my parents experienced a crisis and asked me to help them move back to North Carolina to start a new business. I was driven by duty but torn by my devotion to Mike. Duty won the war, and I moved.

Within six months Mike showed up at my door asking me to move back to Georgia and move in with him. I told him I needed time to think about it, but Mike was a quick decision maker. With him, you made a decision and went with it, immediately. When I hesitated, he left, as in, "I am going to the airport" left. I tried to chase him down to no avail, but later that evening he showed up at my door again. We were each other's drug, and no matter how much either of us acted like we weren't addicted, we always came back. We told my parents (who subsequently didn't speak to me for six months), rented a U-Haul, and headed for Georgia. Mike later asked me to marry him. Maybe my dreams were finally coming true!

A few months into our engagement a mutual friend of ours asked to move in with us because she was going through a separation from her husband. We had all been friends in high school, and against our better judgment she moved in with us. Mike's warm nature drew her attention, and she began flirting with him. At first I believed it was innocent; after all, she was going through a hard time and needed friends. It didn't take long for my song to change. She was coming on to him in my own home, a lot. Ask any man alive, a woman who wants you can be hard to resist.

I was devastated. I couldn't breathe and experienced my first, full-on, anxiety meltdown. This hurt touched on such a deep place of insecurity that for the first time in my life I began believing the lie that I was not enough and that I was inadequate as a woman.

As a result, I moved out and we called off the wedding. But after the shock had worn off, my pain of losing him became much greater than the hurt of his betrayal. I wanted him back, I wanted his love. I wanted to be wanted.

Within 30 days after I moved out, he was back at my door asking me to come back and marry him. I said yes, and we were married on October 11, 1986. I bought into the lie that I should pretend that bad things have never happened.

The greatest joys of my life have come from Mike and me having our two sons. I did not know I was capable of such love until God gave me Blake and Hunter. I would give my life for them without a second thought. However, for Mike and me the challenges were far from over, and my perfect little life was not so perfect under the surface.

My pattern of doing anything and everything to please Mike was exhausting. I continued believing the lie that I needed to please others in order to be okay with myself. He had become very successful in business, and along with that came the financial benefits of success. The tragedy of wealth, however, is that you can believe that everyone always expects you to have it together After all, you've done well and you aren't stressed about money, so why do you have any right to be unhappy. While I may have learned the mask of isolation very young from a mother who never, and I mean never, shared one word with anyone about the mistreatment she received at the hands of my father, I perfected my mask of togetherness during our early years as a family.

This lie trapped me into believing that I couldn't share my pain with anyone. The problem with masks is that they never allow you to deal with what's real. It was like putting a Band-Aid on cancer. I kept on covering, I kept on hiding, I kept on pretending.

Whoever conceals their sins does not prosper, but the one who confesses and renounces them finds mercy. Proverb 28:13

Despite my efforts to pretend things were okay and to not allow anyone to know about what had become a tangled mess of sexual dysfunction and relational catastrophe, God would not leave me alone. He kept drawing me closer to Him through prayer and even when I wanted Him to leave me alone, I knew that He wouldn't. This kind of patient love I understood, maybe it was the only kind of love I understood, and it was how God came to me. He spoke what I could hear and in a way I could hear it. Unfortunately, the more I heard from Him, the more that seemed to draw me into conflict with the choices I was making.

One night in particular, Mike and I had gotten into an argument, and I was left alone in our room. I reached over and took my Bible, held it close to my chest, and just rocked back and forth. Through my tears I opened the pages and began to read. The Bible had fallen open to Jeremiah 15:19-21.

Therefore, thus says the Lord, "If you return, then I will restore you— before Me you will stand; And if you extract the precious from the worthless, you will become My spokesman. They for their part may turn to you, but as for you, you must not turn to them. Then I

will make you to this people a fortified wall of bronze;
and though they fight against you, they will not prevail
over you; for I am with you to save you and deliver you"
declares the Lord. "So I will deliver you from the hand of
the wicked, And I will redeem you from the grasp of the
violent."

I had no clue of the context or basis for what I was reading, but as I read, I was immediately comforted. I completely embraced God's promise to restore me. I was struck by the phrase 'that I would stand before Him, to extract the precious from the worthless,' because I absolutely believed the lie that I was worthless.

And then "that I will become His spokesman," well, that was simply a faint heart's desire, but His promise comforted me nonetheless. What was so great about this passage was that it not only included comfort for me, it gave instructions. At that point I knew that no matter what, I was not supposed to turn back, even if there was a fight. God promised that if I would stand firm, He would not let evil prevail over me, that He would be there to save me and to deliver me. I clung to this truth like a lifeline. The trouble, though, was that I also chose to believe that I could handle the mounting issues within my marriage with just God and me. I honestly didn't want to bother anyone. I was also ashamed, embarrassed, and very, very confused. My isolation encouraged the lie of belief that I can deal with my problems with just God and me. Something had to give, but it would be many more years before the dam broke.

Over the next twenty years, we continued our pattern of love and hurt. Thankfully, God was working on our behalf and led us to a church, First Baptist Church

Woodstock (FBCW). I found such purpose and joy in service; it silenced the painful, unanswered questions of my heart and allowed me to pour out into something good. I also connected with some amazingly Godly women who began mentoring me. Bonnie and Debbie were sent from God for me. I was a Christian who desperately needed saving.

I first met Debbie Hale when our sons were on the same baseball team. Debbie is a spitfire sweetheart. She's a servant and one of the most genuine people I've ever met. God knew I needed a Debbie in my life. We became friends and connected at church. I can remember Mike specifically saying to Debbie "I can really see a change in Ann since you two are spending so much time together." Debbie and I became close friends; we worked out together and spent time at church together. She encouraged me to get involved, and I did. My draw toward church was becoming stronger because I now had a friend to share it with.

Bonnie Oliff Tucker and I were high school friends. She had been my big sister in cheerleading and had remained a voice of encouragement in my life. When we started attending FBCW, we reconnected. When problems at home began to escalate, I followed my pattern of retreat, and she began reaching out to me in the spring of 1998. She kept on inviting me to return to her Sunday School class. I avoided her calls and ignored her invites. On December 14, she died of cancer. At her funeral, the pastor gave an invitation and I rededicated my life to Christ.

After rededicating my life, I became more active in choir and serving. I was determined to get the boys to church regularly and serve in any way I possibly could. The more I learned and grew, the more challenging things became at home. Mike was coming to church with me, but I wanted him to know and feel what I was learning and experiencing the same as I was. But in my newfound spiritual excitement, Mike only felt pushed and judged. And so what did I do? I did what I always did, I kept our challenges quiet. I tried to be what I thought Mike wanted me to be, and I also tried to be a good Christian.

I have since come to realize that there are many, many women (and men for that matter) who struggle with wanting a spouse to experience faith the way they are experiencing it, and wrestle with knowing how to be supportive and genuine without coming across as judgmental. There is no magic bullet for this. Unfortunately, I was given some bad, albeit well-intentioned, spiritual advice. I chose to believe the lie that my involvement in church was detrimental to my marriage. So I stepped away from church.

Not long after, our family moved further into North Georgia, and going to the same church was no longer an option. For the first time in my life, I felt like God had abandoned me. He had taken me away from a place of refuge and purpose, and I felt alone. Then God clearly spoke directly to my heart that day and said, "I am the one who wants to feed you. The Church is My Body but I want you to learn to know ME and be loved by ME." God showed me that day that I needed to learn to feed myself. Immediately I started trying to figure out how I was going to learn more about God, to get closer to God, and also how to please Mike by not doing it on the weekends when he wanted our family to be together. I remembered Debbie telling me about Precept Ministries. We were only about 45 minutes from Chattanooga, so I looked them up on the Internet and signed up for one of their women's conferences. While I was at the conference, I learned about their weekly pilot Bible studies and that was it! I could come on Tuesdays while Mike was at work and learn to study God's Word. I did it, and the more I studied, the hungrier I got! What I didn't know at the time was that this was all part of God's desire to draw me closer and closer to Him. It was to prepare me for that day in May of 2012 when He became more important than my marriage and family, when I would finally get to the point that no one would be able to separate me from loving, serving, and dedicating my life to Him.

After years of being fed by Precept, I started looking for ways to pass on to others what I had been learning. Yes, things at home were still a mess, but I had this burning desire in my heart to pour into others. We eventually relocated to Marietta, and we started attending FBCW again. Pastor Johnny and his wife Janet became dear friends to Mike and me, and I shared with them upon one occasion that I would like to teach in some capacity. In case you don't know, never mention to your Pastor that you want to teach a Bible study unless you are in fact ready to teach right away. He helped me get started as a Precept teacher and actually came to my first class, a study on Genesis, to support me and encourage the work God was doing in me.

I was coming alive in teaching. Other people were being transformed, I was mentoring, helping disciple in leadership, and birthing new classes to teach using the

Precept method. But things weren't getting better at home; in fact, they were getting worse, much worse. Our boys were grown and could no longer be the buffer that kept us together. Despite the fact that we still desperately loved each other, the cracks in our relationship were becoming ravines. I knew we could not take much more. I couldn't take much more. But long before there can be healing, there must be truth, and truth is what I needed and feared. This need led me to the events on May 29, it was time for truth; God knows I needed it.

> *It is for freedom that Christ has set us free. Stand firm, then, and do not let yourselves be burdened again by a yoke of slavery. Galatians 5:1*

May 30, 2012—still in Israel

I. Am. Mortified.

I want to hide. I want to disappear. Last night I told my Pastor and his wife the truth about my marriage, and now I have no idea what to do or what to say. Do I act normal now? What does that even look like? I am on vacation with my son; he knows we have had our challenges, sure, but this is our mess, not his. Oh, I wished I had kept my mouth shut and never written that stupid note....

These (and many others) are the thoughts that plagued me as I began our next day of "vacation." During our first outing of the day I tried to remain as inconspicuous as possible, but my raw emotional state eventually bubbled to the surface. As I walked away from the group to try and compose myself, my pastor came and offered words of wisdom, "Ann, we love you and Mike. We will do whatever we can to help you get the help you need. You're not alone." I was still so shaky with this new ground of honesty that I don't even remember how I responded, but I do remember that I resolved in my heart that I would not go down without a fight, WE would not go down without a fight. After a few minutes to compose myself, I returned to the group with a fresh resolution to try and enjoy the days I had with my son and to absorb as much of God's truth as my soul would allow.

A few days later, I was baptized in the Jordan River. I knelt in the same waters that had once covered my Savior. While I knew we had a long way to go, it was as if the Spirit of God was washing me clean once again, reminding me that I am not defined by my choices or by being together; I am called His beloved, and to Him, I am pleasing. The truth was coming out, and God was at work. Mike was saved on June 17, 2012. This time, I DID hear the angels singing:

There is therefore now no condemnation for those who are in Christ Jesus. Romans 8:1

Therefore, if anyone is in Christ, he is a new creation. The old has passed away; behold, the new has come. 2 Corinthians 5:17

But you are a chosen race, a royal priesthood, a holy nation, a people for his own possession, that you may proclaim the excellences of Him who called you out of darkness into His marvelous light. Once you were not a people, but now you are God's people; once you had not received mercy, but now you have received mercy. 1 Peter 2:9-10

Pastor Johnny remained true to his word, and we began intensive counseling and therapy both as a couple and as individuals. Meeting with professionals who were equipped to help us was imperative. Mike and I had both made choices, and it was time for me to accept responsibility for my part and own it. The good thing about bringing things into the light is that once you start, bringing the truth out gets easier and easier. It is no coincidence that Jesus tells that truth brings freedom—it does! It also brings reality, and this requires practical help to deal with and muddle through.

Let us then with confidence draw near to the throne of grace, that we may receive mercy and find grace to help in time of need. Hebrews 4:16

We were recommended to a therapist, Robbie Goss, in Florida who began working with us to unravel the lies. It became quickly apparent that I needed a separate therapist to just focus on my issues while Mike worked with Robbie. I began working with Susan Adams, confessing, explaining, and revealing things that I had never told anyone before. She helped me to get comfortable and feel safe with the process.

During our first session, I began pouring out the details of my life, and with barely any emotion at all, I gave her specifics about abusive situations that had taken place that were very painful. Having developed the coping skills, disassociation and denial, I was disconnected from them at that point. I had no ability to feel any emotion about them because I had kept them more than an arm's length from me. It was if I was describing someone else's past, not mine. Susan was crying, and when I looked up she asked me why I had no tears for what I had been through. I couldn't really explain it, but they just weren't there. All my years of believing the lie that I could handle my pain alone had cut me off not only from others but also had cut me off from myself. After that initial encounter, I began working to speak openly with our therapists. Slowly but surely my emotions began to come to life, and my tears eventually returned.

> *You (God) keep track of all my sorrows. You have collected all my tears in your bottle. You have recorded each one in your book. Psalm 56:8*

The journey of counseling can be an awful and incredible experience. Make no mistake, it is not easy to face your fears, but there were so many lies that I had come to believe, so many patterns of broken thinking, so much hurt that had entangled itself into my heart and my marriage that I knew my only hope was to press on towards truth. So one step at a time we called out the lies, revealed them for what they were, and focused on the truth.

I was led to do an exercise called Lies and Truth where I could write down the lie and the truth in a format and repeat it every day for 60 days until I had the truth committed to memory. When I was tempted to believe one of my lies, I would immediately think of the truth and base my responses on truth rather than the lie.

The format: I reject the lie that_____ in the name of Jesus. The truth is_____ .

Practically speaking, Robbie would confront me when he identified a lie and would basically say to me, "you are a Precept teacher right?" Then he would proceed to ask me "What does God's Word have to say about that?" Then I would proceed to lower my head and tell him that I knew the truth but had not applied it. Or I would say, "No, I don't know. Tell me what His Word has to say about that." Below is an excerpt of my list:

LIE: It's okay to rescue others from their consequences
TRUTH: I need to allow others to experience consequences in order to help them grow

LIE: I need to over-extend myself in order to prove my value
TRUTH: I need to maintain lifestyle balance in order to be at peace with God, others and myself

LIE: I am not enough; I am inadequate
TRUTH: I am wonderfully made and adequate for every good work

LIE: My feelings are not important
TRUTH: God values me and gave me my feelings to warn and protect me

LIE: I need to pretend this didn't happen
TRUTH: I need to face my pain, maintain boundaries, and receive healing for damaged emotion

LIE: My value comes from pleasing others
TRUTH: My value comes from the Lord; He loves me unconditionally

LIE: I don't want anyone to think I am special
TRUTH: I am a unique, unrepeatable miracle of God

LIE: I can handle my problems alone
TRUTH: I need to value myself enough to seek support

As for combating isolation, I forced myself to reach out to at least ten friends and meet with them to be transparent about what I was going through. For the first time in my life, I was being honest with others, and in return, they began being more honest with me. I started seeing God answer some of the prayers I had been praying for years. Yes, there is freedom in the truth, but there is POWER in the truth as well.

Therefore, confess your sins to one another and pray for one another, that you may be healed. The prayer of a righteous person has great power as it is working. James 5:16 ESV

Warning: I did have to carefully and slowly be transparent with a few friends to make sure that this was a type of relationship they were up for. First, some people aren't safe to share intimate details of your life with, and second, some people don't want to know you that well. They just don't want to hear someone's junk and that's okay.

Mike and I continued to be counseled and coached by Robbie for two years. Together, we began learning to build healthy intimacy and closeness. One of Robbie's practices for us is a daily six-second kiss. And the more we chose intimacy with God, the closer we grew in intimacy with each other. God always exceeds our expectations of His blessings. Always.

Now to him who is able to do immeasurably more than all we ask or imagine, according to his power that is at work within us, to him be glory in the church and in Christ Jesus throughout all generations, for ever and ever! Amen. Ephesians 3:20-21

Just a few short months later, I sensed the Lord leading me to start a ministry. It was an intense desire that I could not understand, but I also couldn't get rid of it. So, with Mike's blessing, I stepped out in faith. I began praying for a name for the ministry, and because it was as though grace has been poured into every step of my past journey, *In Grace* was the perfect name to represent our future. I continue to teach Sunday School and have incorporated a leadership coaching program (Discovery Leadership Coaching) into our instruction for Bible Study leaders. I now co-host a local Atlanta talk show, *The Christian View*, and am currently pursuing a Master of Arts in Leadership at Southeastern Baptist Theological Seminary. It is as if God has poured open the floodgates of opportunity and I want nothing more than to proclaim His amazing grace to the world.

God started me on this journey with *five-seconds of courage,* now Mike and I continue forward each day with a six-second kiss. Some days the kiss is better (and longer) than others, but we are growing, we are committed, and we remain in love. God is continuing to work in us. Of course there is no such thing as a perfect marriage. But when new troubles arise, we both know that He will provide *five more seconds of courage* for us to face those challenges together.

About the Author

Ann is Founder and President of In Grace Ministries, a non-profit organization dedicated to strengthening believers in the Word, equipping ministry leaders to serve, and empowering women and children at risk. In order to fulfill this mission, Ann invests time both locally and internationally, teaching Bible studies, training ministry leaders, and partnering with organizations that rescue and restore victims of neglect and abuse.

Over the past 10 years, Ann has served as an advocate for foster children and families through her work on both state and local boards and has led fundraising projects to support these efforts. Ann is the Director of Precept Study Groups and the Discovery Leadership Coaching program at First Baptist Church in Woodstock, Georgia and is continuing to strengthen her skills by pursuing a Master of Arts in Leadership at Southeastern Baptist Theological Seminary.

On top of being a wife, a mom, a speaker, and leading a ministry, Ann co-hosts a local Atlanta talk show, *The Christian View*. Despite her busy schedule, you can find her spending quiet moments with the Lord, hanging out with her husband, boys and their families, working out, writing, reading, enjoying dear friends, and learning to live IN GRACE.

Ann's new book, Five Seconds of Courage will be released in 2015. For more information visit www.InGraceMinistries.org.

The Storm

Amber Hatcher-Weaver

I never would have imagined that a year and a half into marriage, at the young ages of twenty-two and twenty-one, my husband and I would find ourselves in the midst of a storm. The hardest part of getting caught in the middle of a storm is that, no matter which direction you look, nothing is visible except the storm. Our storm surrounded us in the form of depression and anxiety, and caused my husband, Matthew, to experience what some might call a nervous breakdown.

Matthew and I were married in the month of January. Four seasons came and went. Another May rolled around, and things began to spiral out of control. At the age of only four years old, Matthew found his father dead as he attempted to wake him up one morning. His dad, born with a heart defect, had died in his sleep. Experiencing such intense trauma at an early age had a profound effect on the rest of his life. Normally a compassionate, caring, and charismatic person, Matthew began acting very unlike himself; he wasn't sleeping or eating well. He was frequently very anxious, and he began to be paranoid, saying strange things to me and other family members. For weeks, the chaos and frantic tension slowly mounted around us in our home until it was a tangible presence.

I came home from work on a Monday evening to find Mathew in a great mood. After an intense, and to be honest, insane couple of weeks, I thought things were finally looking up. He welcomed me home. We talked. I discovered that he had taken off of work early that day, but was too exhausted to question him or to try to figure out why. He jumped in the shower, and after a few minutes, I heard him call my name.

I walked into the bathroom. "What, babe?"

He pulled the shower curtain back so that I could see his face, and with a puzzled look asked, "Why are you always so nice to me?"

What? What kind of question was that? Not entirely sure how to answer him, I responded, "Because I love you? And I'm your wife. I'm supposed to be nice."

He closed the curtain and went back to showering. I remember thinking, *Is that what you called me in here for?* A few minutes later, both showered and dressed, he called me again from the bathroom. As he was brushing his teeth, he suggested, "Hey, why don't you go ahead and go to my mom's house. I'll finish getting ready and meet you over there." We had planned to go to his mother's home for dinner. She knew he had been struggling, so as a family we were trying to help each other and make sure he was eating and sleeping. "Could you go ahead and go? I am going to finish up and I will meet you there."

"No, I'll wait for you, " I told him in a matter of fact tone. I didn't want to go without him.

His mood was so great, as he responded, "No, you go on."

Something felt off. *Why did he want me to go ahead without him?* I verbally agreed to do as he requested, with no intention whatsoever of leaving.

I left the bathroom and walked through the living room. The sound of my heels echoed throughout the house as I passed through the kitchen and made my way into the laundry room. I opened and closed the back door leading to our carport, but did not exit. I did not leave the house. While my hand was still on the doorknob, Matthew walked through the kitchen and went into the guest bedroom, directly across from the back door where I stood; it was the only room of the house I had not been in that day. He looked me straight in the eye, then closed the door to the guest room and locked it. *What just happened?* I was completely confused.

I walked straight to the locked door. I put my hand on the door knob, trying to turn it, to open it, to unlock it. Concerned but calm, I said, "Matthew, what's going on? Open the door." My mind was beginning to race. All I could think about was the storm we were in, the chaos that had enveloped our home, and of the strange events that had been happening over the past several weeks. *Yesterday he told me if I noticed anything strange or saw anyone at our house when I drove by, I was NOT to go in, and now he has locked himself in this room. What is in this room? Who is in this room? What is going on?* The thoughts and questions ran together.

Finally his voice interrupted the stream of questions in my mind. "I just want you to go on to my mom's. I am going to read some stuff and work on this song. I just want to work on this for a bit. I want to be alone. Just go ahead and go to my mom's."

I knew his guitars were in there, but still I pleaded, "No. I am not leaving without you. Open the door."

He stayed surprisingly and mysteriously calm as he continued to insist that I go to his mom's without him, and as I continued to refuse to leave him. We went round and round in this manner until finally, in anger I said, "Fine. I'll go!"

I flew out the door, jumped in my car, and backed out of the carport. At the very end of the driveway I heard God say in my heart and in my mind, *Get back in that house.* I knew things were very wrong. I put the car in drive, quickly pulled back up to the house, and walked in through the same door I had just exited.

I called Matthew's name. Once, twice. No answer. The third time I screamed his name.

As calm as could be, his voice came through the door. "What?"

I was angry. "What is going on?" I wanted in that room, and he wouldn't let me in.

He simply said, "Can you pray for me?"

I fired back, "You know what, if you want to pray, you pray. You know how to pray. You can pray just as well as I can. You pray." So he did.

I sat down outside of the locked door. As he prayed, I listened. I was scared and confused. I had known Matthew was struggling beyond what I was equipped to help him with, but I had never fully comprehended the struggle in my own mind. I was scared to death, but I continued to listen to Matthew's prayer. "Lord, thank you for Amber. Thank you for the wife she was to me." I suddenly realized that things in his prayer were in the past tense. He continued to pray intimately, deeply, and with much detail.

Never had I been so thankful to hear "Amen," but the questions were still raging! When I found my voice, I asked, "I don't understand. Why was everything in past tense? Why were you saying I *was* a good wife? Why are you saying all of those things?"

Then his calm voice came once again from the other side of the door. "You are, Amber. You are going to do great things. You are going to live a great life and be happy."

Frustrated, I insisted, "I *am* happy. What are you talking about? Open the door!"

But he wouldn't. And I was scared. I forced myself to think about what I should do, needed to do, or even could do. The decision seemed clear: call his mom. "We need to call your mom. She's expecting us for dinner. I am not going if you're not going, so we need to call and let her know that we aren't going to make it tonight."

He agreed, and asked me to get the phone so that we could make the call. I went into the living room to get our cordless phone. When I returned with it, Matthew had to open the guest room door to grab it. All I could think was *here's my chance to get into that room.* When I tried to wrap my hand around the door so that I could open it, he quickly pulled it shut. I yanked my hand back to keep it from being caught. That was the moment that I knew, beyond a shadow of a doubt, something was terribly wrong.

A kind of calmness washed over me, in spite of this disturbing realization, and I said, "I'm going to lay the phone down, and I am going to walk away. You call your mom and let her know we aren't coming." I placed the phone beside the door and walked into the living room. Once I'd left the doorway, Matthew opened the door, got the phone, and called his mom. I knew if he told her we were not coming, she would be alarmed. I knew no matter what, help was on the way.

"Amber, my mom wants to talk to you." I lifted myself out of his leather recliner in our living room, walked through the kitchen, and reached for the phone. He looked at me. I grabbed the phone and without letting go, Matthew said, "I love you." He kissed me. Both of our hands were still on the phone.

Still scared, confused, and defeated I said, "I love you, too. I don't understand. Why are you doing this?" He didn't answer.

His mom was waiting for me on the phone. I wanted to move away from Matthew. I wanted to be sure he couldn't hear what I was going to say to her, so I went back into the living room and sat in his recliner again. This time I sat on the edge of the seat, causing the recliner to lean forward. When Matthew had been on the phone with his mom, I overheard him tell her that I would still be going to her house for dinner and that he would be there later. That was a red flag to her, so she wasn't surprised when I told her I actually wasn't going to make it. "We're on our way, Amber. You stay there." I assured her I would stay put and wait for them to come over. After we hung up, mental and emotional relief spread throughout my body. I exhaled as I leaned back from my upright position in the chair. Finally, help was on the way.

Just as my back touched the leather, there it was. The noise. The noise that will not leave my head: the gunshot. Louder than the gunshot, though, was the sound of Matthew's body hitting the floor. My body jolted into an upright position. Just as quickly as the tension had left my body when I leaned back in the chair, I found myself perched on the edge of the seat, calling for help.

"9-1-1. What is your emergency?"

I was beginning to hyperventilate.

"I think my husband just shot himself."

"What is your name and address?"

I responded.

"Ma'am, why do you think this?"

"Because he is in our guest bedroom with the door locked. I just heard a gunshot."

"Are you still in the house? You need to get out of the house as quickly as possible."

I could not breathe. The dispatcher was trying to help me.

"Do not hang up the phone Amber. Stay on the phone with me," she insisted over and over.

"We need to call his mom. We need to call his mom."

"Amber, do not hang up the phone."

I am face down kneeling in the front yard. I can see myself. I am wearing a white peasant-type skirt and a sleeveless, black top. The grass is lush and green from recent rain. The phone is beside my head.

I see the ground.

I see my body.

I can't breathe.

I am certain I am about to pass out or throw up, and I'm slowly, desperately praying. "Please, Lord, kill me. Please make me die right now. This cannot be happening." Then I see a familiar face. One of the first responders, a police officer I recognize as a security guard at the bank where I work, has arrived and is walking toward me.

His touch functioned as a vacuum, sucking me right back inside of my body. *No, don't touch me,* I thought. In that moment, I knew this was real. I saw our home. I saw our porch. I saw that the front door was open. He walked toward the porch, and crouched beside our living room window with his gun drawn.

"What are you doing? Why are you waiting and not going in?" He explained to me that he had to wait for backup. As he was explaining, the 9-1-1 dispatcher was still trying to talk to me and ask me questions over the phone. Then I heard sirens, and it hit me: the sirens were coming for me. They were coming to my home. This was my 9/11.

Fire trucks, ambulances, police cars—there were people everywhere. There was so much noise, yet I heard nothing. I remained on the ground, watching the chaos, still not fully comprehending what was happening. Several emergency responders came my way, trying to get me to calm down. It worked in spurts. Every time I would get my breathing calmed, something else would happen, and I would start to hyperventilate again. Then I saw Matthew's mom, Martha, walking towards me.

I saw the look of terror on his mom's face as she came over to me, put her arms around me, and asked, "Amber, what happened?" I don't remember answering her. I didn't know if I could speak. She instantly, without hesitation began to pray, "God, send your angels. Send them so close that we would feel their wings." All I could think was *who is this woman? Her child is in this home, there are people everywhere. Who is this woman that she would stop and pray for me?*

Living in a small town, everyone knows everyone, and news travels fast. Because of what had just happened, my unstable condition, and the probability that friends and family would want to see us, emergency responders thought it would be best if they took me to the hospital. I was on a beta-blocker already, and my heart rate was extremely high. I suppose the hospital seemed like the logical solution. They loaded me into an ambulance, where I continued the vicious cycle of calming myself down only to begin hyperventilating again. I lay on the stretcher, on my back, trying to breathe. One of the paramedics started asking me random questions to make sure I was coherent. "How tall are you?" "Where do you work?"

Martha came over to the ambulance and asked, "Can I ride with her?" She got in. Again, I thought, *who is this woman*? This time, I was irritated that they were helping me and not Matthew.

I looked at her and said, "You don't need to come with me. You need to go in there and help him."

She was crushed, yet strong as she said, "Amber, there is nothing we can do for him anymore. We have to help you now."

Just like that. Every dream we shared, every aspiration we had, everything was gone.

He was gone.

Tears began to stream down my face. The calmness I had felt earlier from the outside of the locked door washed over me again. This time, it came with such a deep hurt that my body couldn't move. It felt like something weighing 1000 pounds had slowly been laid across my chest. Not all at once, but 5 pounds, 10 pounds, 20 pounds, 50 pounds... I was sinking.

The ambulance moved. We were driving to the emergency room. Shortly after I arrived at the hospital, people began to gather. I remember family and friends, pastors and church leaders. My unsettled spirit was so conflicted that, while I didn't want to be alone, I wanted them all to leave. Then it wouldn't have to be real. At some point, I went to the restroom and my mom accompanied me. Out of the blue, I just said what popped into my mind. "Every dream is gone. I will never have his babies."

Matthew was handsome. In fact, he was voted Most Handsome in high school. He had green eyes just like me, but the most beautifully shaped eyebrows and facial structure. I had dreamed of the day I would see our child and how beautiful he or she would be. "It's going to be okay. God has different plans for your life," came her simple reply. It wasn't what I wanted to hear in that moment, but I conceded, "I know."

In reality, I had no idea what God's plan was for me. No one did. Going home that night was not an option, so I stayed with Matthew's mom. I had been given medication to help me calm down and rest, which allowed me to sleep through the night. I woke up the next morning to the sound of people. They had already started coming over to show their support. I lay there praying, *Lord, please just kill me. Please make me die. This can't be real. This can't be my life. I don't want to do this.* I waited for a few minutes, giving God a little time to grant my request, but He didn't. So, even though I didn't want to see anyone, I got up. We had a funeral to plan.

Over the next few days, we experienced an overwhelming outpouring of love from our community. We had a constant flow of support from people because they loved our families, they loved me, they loved Matthew's mom, and they adored Matthew. Hundreds of people came to honor his life. *If only he could have seen how many cared for him.* From food to flowers, we were cared for. But I was numb. Having had nothing but water for several days, I went to the funeral exhausted and weak. So much of it was a blur. It didn't feel real.

Seven days passed; they felt like an entirely different dimension of my life. On the seventh day, almost to the hour of Matthew's death, I received a call from my endocrinologist, whom I had visited earlier that day. She had seen my blood work. I was pregnant.

Shortly before Matthew and I got married, I had been diagnosed with Graves' disease: an immune system disorder that affects the thyroid. My doctor and Matthew had a great relationship working to keep me in line and taking my medicine. I can remember many times when I would stop all medication, because it caused me to gain weight. Matthew would tell on me. As a result of my struggles with the steroids and other medicines, my doctor decided to treat me with radioactive iodine. Because I just had my second treatment two months prior, she was not sure if I should continue with the pregnancy for many reasons, both health and situational. But I was adamant. "If I am pregnant, I am going to have this baby, so you need to figure out what needs to happen. Terminating this pregnancy is not an option." When she saw how firmly I felt about it, she said she would contact nuclear medicine and referred me to a doctor who could treat high risk pregnancy. We ended our conversation and I hung up the phone. "What ifs" flooded my mind. *How could I just be finding this out? What if we had known sooner? If Matthew had known, would things be different?*

My mom's house had become a place where I would go to just kind of be "off the grid." She lived in another nearby town, so I could go there and truly be alone. I was driving back home and as I pulled into town, I automatically turned as if I was going to my house, the house where Matthew and I lived. I broke. I began to weep, sobbing so hard that I could barely see to drive. I had been living with Martha. A widow herself, she understood what it was like and had taken me in as her own. But, for the first time, as I realized that I could not go to *my* home, I felt homeless. It was more than I could bear.

I made my way to Martha's house. She had company. I would keep my head down, greet them in passing, and head straight to my room. As I grabbed a glass of water, Martha caught a glimpse of my face. She knew something was wrong. I went to my room, buried my face in the bed and wept. Not long after, I felt Martha lay her hands on my back. She gently asked what had happened.

I replied, "I just want to be where he is." Everything was wrong, but those were the only words that I could get to come out of my mouth.

With so much wisdom, she softly said, "No, you want him to be where you are."

We understood the language of each other's hearts as we grieved together. On the outside, I worked so hard to smile even when it hurt so that no one else would know my struggles, but that was the day that I finally shut down on the inside.

The first morning of every week while I was getting dressed, I would stand in front of the mirror, put on my makeup, and relive the events leading up to Matthew's death. *What if I had done this? Perhaps I should have done that.* Like a puzzle with missing pieces, I could never make it fit together.

My life had already been completely on display to the public since Matthew's passing, and now to top it all off, I was pregnant. I was happy that Matthew's legacy would continue, and that I would still be connected to him, but how would I raise this child? Satan began to plant seeds of insecurity and doubt. At the same time, God was flooding my mind with meaningful scripture and carrying me through. He had given me a verse before Matthew died, and it was one to which I continued to cling. *Psalm 46:1 God is our refuge and strength, a present help in trouble.*

The discovery that I was pregnant came with its own joys and sorrows. I was both excited and scared, but most of all, I was finally distracted from the trauma that was surrounding me. It was the wakeup call that I needed to get myself together and start taking care of the life growing inside of me. I knew the chances of me getting pregnant had been slim to none at the time, because of my chronic health struggles for the past year. I knew after the two rounds of radioactive iodine, this baby was truly a miracle, and God continued to perform miracles for the duration of the pregnancy.

I was not even fully aware of the magnitude of my situation until I received a letter from the nuclear medicine department. They informed me that the radiation had to be out of my body for at least six months before certain organs began forming in the baby, which happens during the second trimester, in order to minimize the risk of developmental defects. The letter went on to say, "You had a radiation treatment in April and conceived in May. The organs that can be affected develop during the 4th month of gestation. That would be six months, so we believe the radiation will be out of your system and the baby will be fine." Medical personnel I didn't even know were meeting on my behalf to make sure that everything was going well with me and with the baby throughout my entire pregnancy.

I found out I was having a boy. It was a bitter-sweet moment. Picking out the name presented a bit of a challenge, but I knew God had gone before me. The middle name was a no-brainer, Dock. That was Matthew's middle name, a family name, and it's just a great name. I was still undecided on the first name, yet I knew I wanted a biblical name. Then one day it just came to me: Benjamin. Matthew's grandfather's name was Henry Benjamin.

During this time I began to pray, *Lord, I know you speak to us in the womb. So, right now, I want you to begin to prepare this baby for what he is going to have to know one day.* That is still my prayer today: that God will prepare Benjamin for the details of his father's death, and that he will know his life was not a mistake.

Benjamin's birth was also bittersweet. Repeatedly answering the question of "what happened" was overwhelming to me, as was filing for a birth certificate and having to say that the father was deceased. I felt isolated even though I was surrounded by family and friends. I would frequently find myself in a room full of people, yet still feel lonely.

The second morning after delivering Benjamin, I found myself alone in the hospital room. Benjamin was in the nursery. I was so emotional, so empty, and so heartbroken, yet I knew that I had been given a precious gift. I had a new nurse that day. As she entered the room and asked me a question, she immediately saw how distraught I was. I quickly tried to get it together, but it was obvious that I was upset. She did the normal things all of the other nurses had done. Before she left the room, she turned to me and said, "I'm just going to pray that God will send His angels so close to you today that you will feel their wings." I never saw that nurse again.

I brought Benjamin home to the house Matthew and I owned and had lived in when he died. I had worked so hard with my grandmother the Sunday prior to Benjamin's birth to clean and to get it all together so that we would have *our* space. After coming home, the emotions of everything going on in my life began to run extremely high, which caused me to shut down even further. I continued to slip into a place where I became more and more detached. I was very afraid that I was going to do something wrong. *I don't know what to do. I don't know how to love this child. I don't want him to hurt. I have to create a perfect life, be a perfect mom, and protect this precious baby from pain.* The fears were constant. I was utterly unprepared for what was coming. These fears created a distance between this precious child and me.

Many changes occurred during the first few years of Benjamin's life. Before his first birthday, I decided to go back to college. I sold our home and moved back in with Matthew's mom. It was exciting for me to be back with Martha. I felt like I had someone to do life with again. However, it was also difficult, because I was struggling with the compulsive tendencies that were gradually taking over me. This manifested itself in many unhealthy ways, but Martha continued to be gracious. She cared for us. Anytime Benjamin or I needed something, she was there. Her selfless love was like a life vest keeping me from drowning. To everyone on the outside looking in, everything was great. My need for perfection, however, told a different story.

We lived with Matthew's mom for a while, but eventually I felt it was time to take a step toward living on my own again. Benjamin was around two years old, and I was finishing my degree. As we were packing, moving, and unpacking, Benjamin would find pictures and we would go through them together. I would point to pictures of me, and he would respond, "Mama." One evening he saw a picture of Matthew and me, and pointed to Matthew and said, "Daddy." He knew. To be sure, I dragged out old high school pictures of me with other male friends. He did not identify them in any way. He knew! I had routinely prayed the entire time Benjamin was in the womb that God would prepare him to know his story. Benjamin's responses to the pictures served as a visible answer to my prayers.

I remember the first time Benjamin asked me about his dad. He repeatedly watched *The Lion King*, and I began to notice that he would get extremely still during the scene where Simba's dad dies. One day, he asked, "Where is Simba's dad?"

"Heaven," I replied.

Benjamin asked, "Where is my dad?"

"Where do you think he is?" I asked.

"Heaven," he softly said in his innocent toddler voice.

A tear rolled down my cheek. He took his little hand, wiped away my tear, and asked, "What is that? Are you crying?"

I told him I was, and quickly got it back together. That was the end of it. It was the first time the two of us actually had a conversation about his dad being in heaven. It was also the last for quite some time. I made sure we went right back to our perfect little world where we didn't talk about dads who were in heaven or anything else that might cause pain. I knew it was unhealthy, but that didn't change anything.

Despite the joy this moment of connection with my son brought, I continued to get even worse. I graduated from college, and we moved to McKinney and then to Plano where I had taken jobs. Even though I had longed to be away from everyone, moving away from my family only intensified my struggles. Three-year-old Benjamin started struggling too. In order to get him to go to sleep, every night I would go into his room and lay down with him at bedtime. He would lift his hand in the air, and as he would fall asleep, his arm would drop, causing him to wake up. He was getting no sleep. He was sick all the time. We needed help.

Benjamin began seeing a therapist who utilized play therapy methods with him. Through the course of these sessions, Benjamin's therapist was able to discover the underlying issue. "Amber, he's afraid that something is going to happen to you and that he'll be left with no one."

This was a truth I had a hard time wrapping my head around. Benjamin and I never talked about anything that happened with his dad. I worked tirelessly to make sure everything in our lives was as guarded as possible. I was careful not to be emotional in front of him. The life I was creating was supposed to be a great one. So why was my son struggling with this overwhelming fear? Then it hit me: I wasn't doing something right. "You have to be real with him, Amber. He may not be grieving the loss of the Matthew you knew, but he certainly has to grieve the loss of a dad. He doesn't have a dad and other kids do, so he notices he is different." His therapist's explanation shattered the world I had worked so hard to create. This grief and struggle was my son's reality.

That was the push I needed to begin therapy myself. I worked closely with a Christian counselor who also referred me to a psychiatrist. I had never been to one of "those" doctors. Counselors were fine, but this was out of my comfort zone. When I began telling my story and all that had happened, his response was, "Wow. This could be a Lifetime movie." The realization that nothing about my situation was normal began to truly set in. I was diagnosed with Post-Traumatic Stress Disorder (PTSD) and Obsessive-Compulsive Disorder (OCD). Both of these things were manifestations of the tragedy I had lived. The diagnoses finally gave names to the issues I'd been battling since Matthew's death.

In the moments right after Matthew died, I had felt so close to the Lord. There was a strong spiritual connection as He heard me in the valley of my distress and joined me there. However, as time passed, I began to digress, to detach from the relationship God and I shared, and I distanced myself from the Lord. I was still wrestling. I could not get a strong grasp on anything. Satan had come to kill, steal, and destroy, and he was doing a pretty good job of it. Out of desperation for my child to be healthy mentally and physically, I surrendered: *Lord, I don't know what to do or where to turn. I need your help. Show me what I need to do.*

Benjamin's therapist suggested we move closer to family in order to keep us from being so isolated. We would have more support that way, and perhaps Benjamin having more people in his life would feel more secure. I started saving money for the move right away. On June 2nd, exactly five years from the day Matthew died, I left my job and the security of the world I had created. I picked Benjamin up from his preschool and we walked hand in hand with five balloons to the park beside our apartment. He let the balloons go one at a time. With each release Benjamin was connecting in some way to the father he would never know, but to me each balloon represented years of loss. While I was thankful for the promise and hope of heaven, and that Benjamin and I were communicating about this, it was still a reminder of what life was not.

A week later, we made the move to my mother's house in the tiny town of Wolfe City, TX. It was there that

Benjamin began to instantly thrive. He loved being close to his grandparents again. We were surrounded with family and friends, and we found rest...in a way. I was not sleeping much, but when I did, I would sometimes have beautiful, vivid dreams in which God would provide me with amazing, incredible gifts. I had a couple of these dreams during pregnancy, and had always longed to have more. After the move, I finally had another dream. I was getting to see Matthew again as I slept. The very last dream of this nature that I had was in early September:

Matthew and I are at the Old Concord Baptist Church. Above the altar, there is a sign that reads, "Jesus Christ is the Head of this Church." I am sitting next to Matthew, who is wearing a blue shirt, my favorite shirt. His body is glorified. He is radiant. I know he is not of this world. I am weeping. The service is drawing to a close, and I know once it ends, Matthew will have to go back to Heaven. As we sit in the pew, he puts his arm around me and draws me near. He leans over and whispers in my ear. "Amber, you are going to be okay." He kisses me on the cheek and we worship together. Church ends. We stand up and walk down the aisle. He stops and does not exit the sanctuary. I can't leave him. We embrace and as I look into his eyes, I know he is right, I am going to be okay.

I woke up and knew it would possibly be the last dream of its kind that I would have of him. God was moving and things were changing. I knew in my heart that Benjamin and I were going to be okay.

God would continue to work and ultimately restore what Satan had stolen. For me, part of that restoration has been to understand more about the seriousness of depression and the reality that it is a real illness that claims lives daily. It was an honor to be Matthew's wife, and to have been chosen to walk through this storm with him. I am thankful for so many wonderful memories of our time together in this world. While there are days that my wounds still feel open, I know that it is God, and God alone, who has the power to heal the brokenhearted and to bind up their wounds. He has done that for me. It is in the darkest nights that light shines the brightest. My hope is that through this story, others will see the light of Jesus Christ. My prayer has long been, *Lord, this is your story. Take it and use it. Let it be a story that brings glory to you, even in the darkest of memories and places.* Matthew's life was not defined by his death, just as my life is not defined by the tragedies of my past. Our lives are defined only by the grace of God.

About the Author

Amber Hatcher-Weaver is an entrepreneur, writer and public speaker. She is currently working to complete her memoir which provides insight into the tragedy, wrestling, and restoration she experienced. It is a compelling story.

Amber is the owner of two franchises focused on health and wellness. She is a certified personal trainer and health coach. She holds a Bachelor of Business Administration degree with a major in Human Resource Management from Texas A&M University-Commerce.

Amber and her husband, Barry have three children; Harlan, Benjamin and Olivia. They reside in Commerce, Texas where they are active members of a local church. Amber has a passion for strengthening communities, empowering leaders and inspiring women. She lives out that passion daily through her work and by serving in several non-profit organizations.

To learn more about Amber and information on her upcoming book, or to contact her for speaking engagements, please visit www.amberhatcherweaver.com.

Jehovah is Generous

Kathrine Lee

You have to come with me to the lake. Nancy told me. She wanted to meet up with her boyfriend, but he was at his friend's lake house. My job was to keep the friend company. He was from the great, big, one-stoplight town of Willis, Texas. I was not interested.

Who wants to drive all the way out to the lake to meet some hick from Willis? I'm going to need some alcohol just to get through the evening, I joked. Nancy knew I didn't drink.

Two hours later, we got to the lake. The minute her boyfriend showed up, Nancy disappeared. Then Michael arrived. I took in the view from my little, blue VW bug: Wranglers tucked into cowboy boots, giant belt buckle, no shirt, and a cowboy hat. It just didn't get more hick. He strode up to my car, gave a spit of his tobacco for effect, and greeted me. *I understand you didn't want to meet some hick from Willis?*

The truth is, Michael wasn't like that at all. He didn't even own any of those clothes. When he heard what I had said, he had collected the outfit from all of his friends just to give me a hard time. I was smitten. He took me down to the boat, and offered me a margarita. *I also understand you need some alcohol to get through this evening?* Once more he called me on my stuff. We spent the evening listening to music and enjoying the beauty of the lake. It was so easy to spend time with him, almost as if I had known him my whole life. I didn't take a single sip of that margarita, but I was in love.

After that, for a year and a half, we were inseparable. No one said Michael without also saying Kathrine. We had our problems just like anyone else. Both of us came from homes withbroken families. Michael struggled with feelings of repressed sadness and anger, while I spent all of my time trying to be good enough. Yet, despite Michael's demons and my broken pieces, somehow we were weaving our messes together to create something special...until I got the phone call. Michael had been arrested.

He had been secretly living another life: selling drugs, doing drugs, and being with other women. I was shattered. It was like I didn't know him at all. I drove out to see him at the same lake house where we met. He sat on the porch with his head hung low, bruises on his wrists from the handcuffs. He couldn't even look at me.

He got into rehab, and that was hard on both of us. I visited him often. They told me that he only wanted to get better for me, that I was the other drug in his life, and that he needed to be free of everything on which he depended. They asked me to step back for his sake. I would try, and then would miss him so much that I would come back. It was a vicious cycle for both of us.

For another year and a half we tried to make it work. I moved away to college, and he moved with me. I suppose we thought that physically relocating would mean that we could leave our problems behind. But Michael couldn't break away from the world in which he had become so entangled, and I was attempting to fill my inward emptiness with him. One day, a girl came up to me and asked me if I was Michael's girlfriend. When I told her yes, she told me that he had taken her on a date the night before. At that moment, I finally reached my limit. I couldn't take it anymore.

I called my mom to come get me and take me home. She came all the way from California where she was living to get me. Every waking moment of that twenty-plus hour drive from Texas to California, I cried my nineteen-year-old heart out. Despite everything, I still loved him. When Michael begged me to come back to Texas to visit, I tried. I could see that he still loved me, but that nothing had changed in his life. I was only there for a day before I turned around and went home again. I just couldn't do it.

Shortly after I got back to California, I found out I was pregnant. My dad stepped into my life in a way that he never had before. *Do you want to see the kind of life you are going to have with this boy? I will cut you off financially. Let me show you the kind of place you will live in at age nineteen with a baby. You deserve more than this.* I was overwhelmed by my father's attention and protection, a feeling that I had craved as a child. He stepped in like the hero of my story, ready to do whatever it took to resolve this problem for me. I think it was his own experience of being unwanted and given up for adoption as a child that made my father feel so strongly about what needed to be done in my situation. He wanted me to get an abortion.

My mom was completely against it. Michael couldn't leave Texas because he was still in trouble with the law, but he sent me a ring and asked me to marry him. He and my mother were planning a wedding. And there I was, stuck in the middle: my dad trying to "protect" me for the first time in my life, my mom taking me to see the heartbeat of my baby, and Michael making a plan for our life all the way from Texas.

My dad's voice won. I'll never forget walking into the abortion clinic with his arm around me. The screaming protesters outside of the clinic were quiet as we walked past, silenced by my dad's huge frame and steely stare. It was the strangest feeling. It felt so good to have my father protecting me, but his solution felt so wrong. I had never felt safer around my father, but he was leading me towards death.

I called Michael. *There is no child. There is no wedding. I never want to speak to you again.*

I can't describe the emptiness. I literally lay on the ground in my room for two days straight with the physical symptoms of the decision I had made. But the emotional emptiness was so much worse, like my soul had been ripped out. The reality hit me that life had been taken from me, and it had been my choice to allow it to happen.

I forced my mind to take over, to justify, and to move on—or so I thought. I married the next person that I dated. Once again, I chose someone with a difficult past. Neither of us knew how to love in a healthy way. In my mind, I didn't have any sense of self-worth to want or expect anything more than what he offered me: attention. Because neither of us knew what healthy love was supposed to look like, we chose to marry based on convenience and circumstance. Yet, even out of that brokenness we were blessed with two beautiful children: Corryn and Logan.

My life was a mess. My husband and I were just two people coexisting and trying to play house. I was needy and desperate for love, and he had no idea how to give that to me. In my grief and emptiness, I built a prison out of my own body. I weighed 330 pounds. I was not living I was just existing. Then, my already fragile world was shaken when I found out that my friend, Kelly, who was nine months pregnant, had suffered an aortic aneurism. She and the baby both died. That was the day that literally drove me to my knees.

I challenged God. *If you are the God that I believed in as a child—if you are the God that is supposed to love us, where have you been? I need you to show up and prove that you are real.* In that moment, my eyes were opened to what my world really looked like. God had not abandoned me; it was I who had left him behind. In all of my troubles, I had looked to everything except the one thing that could truly save me.

As I struggled back to my feet, I—Kathrine Nadine— was overwhelmed with a sense of pure hope. I hadn't been myself for so long. I didn't look like myself, feel like myself, or act like myself. But in that moment, God made my identity abundantly clear to me. The name Kathrine means "pure" and the name Nadine means "hope." Only in God could I be my true self. Only in God could I have pure hope for a future that was greater than the present.

I began my journey back towards emotional, physical, and spiritual wellness. I lost weight. My children and I began attending church, something I hadn't done since I was a little girl. God put coworkers and friends in my life that challenged me and mentored me in my young faith. My friend, Steve, taught me that there was a difference between calling oneself a Christian and having a personal relationship with Christ. The idea of a personal relationship with God had been a foreign concept to me up until that point. Another mentor asked me if I owned a Bible in a version that was easy for me to understand. All I had at that point was the King James Version. Later that same day, I found a new Bible in an easier translation on my doorstep. I was filled with a curiosity about God's word and began devoting daily time for prayer and study. I wrote down scriptures that stood out to me and asked God to help me apply His truth in my daily life. Through scripture, I began to understand that transformation neither happens immediately, nor because of my own abilities, but rather over time through the power of God and His word applied in my life.

Then God gently began to take me on a journey to deal with my past. I grieved for my baby—an action I had previously refused to allow myself. As I dove deeper into scripture, I found Deuteronomy 30:15,19: "See, I set before you today life and prosperity, death and destruction... Now choose life, so that you and your children may live", and I was tenderly reminded that I had chosen death. I asked for God's forgiveness, and I was blessed with the hope of getting to see my baby again someday. God spoke to my heart that my baby was a boy, and that his name was Joshua. I knew that eventually I would have to ask for Michael's forgiveness, and I began to pray for God to reveal the right time for me to do so.

Even with all of the good changes in my life, it was not enough to save my marriage. I had hoped that turning my life around would change things in our relationship. I didn't want a divorce, but my husband was done and wanted out. *I don't love you anymore and I don't think I ever did.*

Those words began a very trying time in my life. The enemy of my soul wanted me to believe that I was unworthy of love. But the truth came to me through God's word: "For I am convinced that...[nothing] will be able to separate us from the love of God that is in Christ Jesus our Lord," Romans 8:38-39. I knew my identity in God was secure. Being a single parent was hard; I remember weeping in frustration one night as I took out the trash because I didn't have someone to help me with even the simple tasks. I experienced the sensation of being alone, but was never lonely, because the emptiness in my heart was filled by God. I know that God was the one who completed our family during those years.

After much healing, I finally began to date again. One day while journaling, God put on my heart that it was time to call Michael and ask for his forgiveness. I assumed that I must be ready to put closure on that chapter of my life so that I could move on and get serious with my current relationship. So finally, after fifteen years, I picked up the phone with shaking hands and called Michael. I left a simple message on his answering machine. *The next time I'm in Houston on business I would really like to take you and your wife out to dinner—I have something I would like to talk to you about.*

I heard nothing for three days. I figured that his wife had found the message and erased it. I couldn't blame her. Then I got a phone call from Michael. *You are not going to believe this. I just got home from California. I was there looking for you.* God had prompted both of our hearts to seek reconciliation at the same time.

Michael had been walking a path of healing that was strikingly similar to mine. Michael's marriage had also ended. When I asked him why, he explained to me. *Kathrine, the day you called me and told me there was no wedding and no baby, part of my heart shut down. I never gave my wife access to that part of my heart. I emotionally starved her. She found love and attention somewhere else.*

During our years apart, Michael had also seen his need for God in his life. He gave his pain and his life to the Lord while attending a conference with some co-workers. It was amazing to see the parallel paths that we had been walking in those 15 years.

When we agreed to meet, I felt that it was for the purpose of being able to move on with my life. Michael, however, had different ideas. When he received my message on his answering machine, he immediately called his mother and sister. *I am back in touch with Kathrine, and I am going to marry her someday.*

Michael flew to California, and we met for dinner. While in the restaurant, I asked for his forgiveness and told him about baby Joshua. He wept so hard that we had to leave. He had no idea that my mother had advocated for the life of the baby. That lifted a huge burden of hurt from his shoulders. He had felt deeply wounded because he and my mother had been planning a wedding for us, and he thought that she had encouraged me to have the abortion. He begged to be able to see her and make things right. *Geri, I am so sorry that I was not the man I needed to be, that I put your daughter in the position to have to make such a terrible decision. I want to tell you thank you for trying to save my baby.* My mother saw then what I still failed to see: that Michael had healed, and had finally become a man.

We were both dating other people at the time. Our friendship slowly began again, although rather hesitantly on my side. I still saw actions in Michael's life that I did not feel were in line with the way I knew God wanted him to live. I talked with him about his whole life being a reflection of the grace God had given us. I told him, "I am tired of wanting more for you than you want for yourself." What I didn't know was that I was pushing and challenging my future husband to look more like Christ. Over time, Michael was convicted to fully surrender his life to Christ, instead of the partial dedication he had given before. He quietly realized that he would have to be the man that God was calling him to be in order to be my husband.

Over time, our respective romantic relationships ended. His next business trip to California happened to coincide with a date that I was having surgery. My children were with their father for the weekend, and Michael did not like the thought of me being alone after a surgery. He slept on my couch, and spent the weekend cooking, cleaning, caring for me, and watching movies with me. When he left to fly home, it was like a veil had been lifted from my eyes. I burst into tears. I realized that I was going to miss him, and that I still loved him. The problem was, I had no idea how he felt about me. He called me from the airport. *I just have one thing to ask— Do you miss me?* Five months later, we were married.

The blessings were abundant when Michael and I finally got back together. I didn't understand how we could possibly have such a blessed life in light of our past.

How was it possible that we could live with such joyous love and not be defined by our mistakes? How could such a whole and happy family come out of such brokenness? Michael embraced Corryn and Logan as his own children, even making vows specifically to them at our wedding. We took a family trip instead of a honeymoon so that we could all have time to adjust and bond together.

I felt unworthy of the blessings I was receiving, but above all, I felt unworthy of ever having another child with Michael. However, the grace of God overflowed in our lives and gave us Hannah Grace. Hannah means "grace", so her name is actually Grace Grace. She is our double portion of grace, the gift we do not deserve. Not only did God bring us back together, but He allowed us to have another child together.

Michael and I have now been married for eleven years, and we love each other more each day. Our son Joshua will never be forgotten. He is always in our hearts. In Hebrew, the name Joshua means "Jehovah is generous." God has generously given us a new life, an abundant life showered in the richness of his grace. Our broken family is made whole because of the forgiveness we have received. God can redeem anything. Our lives are living proof of that.

About the Author

Kathrine is a highly sought after life and business strategist. She is the Founder & Co-Creator of The Ultimate Source, a faith-based personal development system that teaches practical application of essential life skills. It was designed so that anyone can experience the abundant life God designed them to live. The Ultimate Source creates a deeper personal connection to God and His Word; therefore, producing more complete satisfaction and fulfillment in life. For more information go to www.theultimatesource.org.

She is also an internationally recognized speaker and has touched millions with her message of hope and transformation. She has worked with corporations like Direct TV, academic institutions such as Lubbock Christian University, and served on the Advisory Board for The Daniel Plan at Saddleback Church. You may recognize Kathrine from one of her appearances on the *Oprah Winfrey Show* or by reading her story in *O Magazine*.

She has established the Pure Hope Foundation (PHF). It's mission is to raise awareness and mobilize action against the sex trafficking industry and to provide second-stage homes where survivors will come for a year or more of continued healing. In addition, PHF will raise funds for the first-stage, front-line ministries that are rescuing, running the safe-houses and stabilizing the girls. Finally, PHF will provide a retreat center and restoration events where pastors and front-line workers can come rest, revive and be equipped to continue to do the work they are called to do. For more information on how you can become involved, visit www.purehopefoundation.com

All profits from this book will go to Pure Hope Foundation.

Afterword

The process of completing this book has been an incredible growth journey for me and has drawn me even closer to my Lord and Savior Jesus Christ. I continually marvel at the way He is so tender and caring to my friends during their darkest moments and walks with all of us on our journeys of faith. If you have questions regarding who this Jesus is, or if you are not really sure what it means to have a personal relationship with Him, I would like to talk with you and share all that He is to me and wants to be for you. No judgment—just a conversation between friends. That is the remarkable thing about Christ, there is nothing you could do that would make Him love you less. And there is no better place to be than in a relationship with Him. Let's talk.

I would also like to hear from any of you who might want to share stories of courageous faith. We have a sense that God might be up to helping us create more of these books. There are many stories that simply need to be told and shared.

And if you want to send a message to any of the authors, you can visit their websites or send to me and I will be happy to forward to them.

You can contact me by visiting: www.kathycrockett.net

About Kathy Crockett

Kathy Crockett, PhD, is a Professor at Lubbock Christian University where she has served since 1997. Her teaching areas include marketing, management, and leadership. She directs the Master of Science in Leadership degree program.

She graduated from Texas A&M University and then completed graduate work at Texas Tech University. She has completed formal training from the Center of Creative Leadership related to Women in Leadership and Executive Coaching. She also completed a year long leadership coaching program with Dr. John Townsend. She has been a facilitator for the Franklin Covey seminar entitled Great Leaders, Great Teams, Great Results.

Kathy develops customized leadership trainings and seminars for students, non-profit organizations, and corporate groups globally. She also is involved as a speaker at churches including women's retreats, ladies bible classes, and servant renewal seminars. Kathy works as an entrepreneur in corporate leadership training, executive coaching, and wellness programs. One of her favorite programs is called Women in Leadership. She has served on various boards and is currently on the board for the Pure Hope Foundation.

Kathy has been married to the love of her life, Steve, for 19 years. They have two daughters, Calley 16 and Maddy 15 who bring so much joy to their lives. They are members of Sunset Church in Lubbock, TX and are involved in missions and youth ministries. For fun, Kathy enjoys running, travelling, spending time with family and friends, and reading.